The Bible Day by Day

May–August 2010

First published in Great Britain in 2010 by Hodder & Stoughton
An Hachette UK company

1

A CIP catalogue record for this title is available from the British Library

ISBN 978 0 340 99541 9

Typeset in Plantin by Avon DataSet Ltd, Bidford on Avon, Warwickshire

Printed and bound in Great Britain
by Clays Ltd, St Ives plc

Hodder & Stoughton policy is to use papers that are natural, renewable and recyclable products and made from wood grown in sustainable forests. The logging and manufacturing processes are expected to conform to the environmental regulations of the country of origin.

Hodder & Stoughton Ltd
338 Euston Road
London NW1 3BH

www.hodderfaith.com

Contents

From the writer of *Words of Life*

Toward Better Vision

There are a number of things that can be done to improve vision clarity. After cataract surgery, two friends now function without their glasses for the first time in decades. If our spiritual sight isn't always 20/20, there are correctives available. If we ask him, God's Spirit will suit the procedure to our need. In one segment of this edition, we will focus on one such means of grace, modelled by Christ – prayer.

Although Jesus prepared the disciples for his crucifixion and resurrection, only after his ascension and the coming of his Holy Spirit at Pentecost did they begin to understand the truth of what he had privately confided to them: 'Blessed are the eyes that see what you see!' (Luke 10:23, *NRSV*).

One person whose sight Jesus restored in stages said that at first men looked like trees walking. We actually do have some traits in common with trees. In this season when trees enter dormancy in the southern hemisphere and send sap to every twig in the north, we remember that our planet depends on the health of our trees. For a fortnight we highlight trees in Scripture.

Our guest writer is Commissioner M. Christine MacMillan. Her biblical perspective challenges us to open cages of injustice and enable people with bound wings to taste freedom and fly again. Poet Maya Angelou writes in her poem, 'Caged Bird', that the caged bird uses the only thing left to it – song:

> The caged bird sings with a fearful trill
> Of things unknown but longed for still
> And his tune is heard on the distant hill
> For the caged bird sings of freedom.[1]

Whether from chapters of Mark's Gospel, several epistles, the little-known book of 1 Chronicles or our Sunday psalm-walk, we seek to catch sight of God's word to our hearts. We pray that as God continues to grant us new insights through his word that we all will see the everyday with new eyes and that our vision of him will improve.

Evelyn Merriam
New York, USA

Abbreviations

AB The Amplified Bible. Copyright © 1965 Zondervan.
CEV *Contemporary English Version.*
JBP *The New Testament in Modern English*, J. B. Phillips, Geoffrey Bles, 1958.
JMT James Moffatt Translation. © 1922, 1924, 1925, 1926, 1935. HarperCollins Publishers.
KJV King James Bible (Authorised Version).
MSG *The Message*, Eugene H. Peterson. © 1993, 1994, 1995, 1996, 2000, 2001, 2002. Used by permission of NavPress Publishing Group.
NCV *New Century Version* © 2005 Thomas Nelson, Inc.
NKJV New King James Bible ®. Copyright © 1982 by Thomas Nelson, Inc. Used by permission. All rights reserved.
NLT New Living Translation. © Tyndale House Publishers, 1996, 1998.
NRSV New Revised Standard Version Bible: Anglicized Edition, © 1989, 1995, Division of Christian Education of the National Council of the Churches of Christ in the USA.
SASB *The Song Book of The Salvation Army*. Copyright © 1986 The General of The Salvation Army.

Intensive Itinerant Instruction

Mark 9–10

Introduction

Not long after Peter's bold confession of Christ as the Son of God, Jesus takes three disciples on an unforgettable overnight mountain retreat. Soon the band travels from that mountain north of the Sea of Galilee, back through Galilee with a stop at seaside Capernaum. With little time left, Jesus instructs the disciples privately on sometimes difficult subjects.

When Jesus leaves Galilee for the last time before his crucifixion, although he moves resolutely toward Jerusalem, he first leads his disciples on a circuitous route south through the Jordan valley into Judea, and east across the Jordan River to the hill country of Perea. His circle of listeners expands as he continues to address important issues and remind his followers of the imperative of sacrificial living.

At the start of the final fifteen-mile uphill trek to Jerusalem, Jesus gives attention to a man in Jericho as he performs the final healing miracle that Mark records. He asks the man, Bartimaeus, the same question he'd asked the disciples – What do you want me to do for you? – and waits for him to articulate his need.

As we journey with Jesus, he allows us to do the same.

Beyond Words

'As they were coming down the mountain, Jesus gave them orders not to tell anyone what they had seen' (v. 9).

The first verse of today's chapter gives the positive side to the final verse of Mark 8 and concludes that section. It may well also introduce the events on the mountain.

What does Jesus mean by 'before they see the kingdom of God come with power'? It might be Jesus' transfiguration; his death, resurrection and ascension; the coming of the Holy Spirit and birth of the Church; Jerusalem's destruction or Christ's second coming. Perhaps the first is most likely, since Mark uses the verse to lead into his account of the transfiguration.

Jesus took Peter, James and John up a high mountain. They may have been preoccupied with the climb, with recent events or even with fear about their fate if and when Jesus' recent prediction of his death was fulfilled. They could not have anticipated what would take place at the summit. Mark says this climb happened six days after Peter's declaration that Jesus was the Christ.

This timeframe could be reminiscent of fulfilment and revelation in the Old Testament. Moses was present on two of those occasions.

God spoke to Moses from Mount Sinai several times. Once he called Moses and Israel's elders to the foot of the mountain. After Moses built an altar there, God called him to ascend the mountain. To those at the foot, the cloud that covered the summit looked like fire.

God's glory settled on Mount Sinai for six days. On the seventh day the Lord called Moses to enter the cloud on the mountain. There God confirmed and detailed his covenant for his people as well as the tabernacle plans (Exodus 24–31).

Although only three disciples were present, Jesus' transfiguration served to further confirm Peter's declaration about him and as a prelude to his Passion. Matthew and Luke also record the momentous event and we perhaps ponder why eye-witness John does not. Perhaps the experience was too full of wonder or precious for him to describe in words, even after Jesus' resurrection.

To ponder:

Does the Holy Spirit guide my speech and silence?

Litany of Everlasting Love

'Give thanks to the God of heaven. His love endures for ever' (v. 26).

Psalm 136 has a unique style. One refrain weaves throughout a series of sentences praising God for who he is and what he's created, and for guiding his people. It concludes every verse: 'His love endures for ever'. The refrain is used in other psalms (such as Psalm 118), but not after every verse, twenty-six times, as it is here. We can imagine a congregation or a choir responding with its affirmation after each statement about God.

The refrain from this psalm was also heard in the time of Ezra when the cornerstone was laid for the rebuilding of the temple and the people recognised anew God's covenantal love for them. The priests and Levites led the dedication service playing horns and percussion, following a pattern from their heritage. Earlier it was heard at the dedication of the first temple and at the placement of the ark of the covenant in a tent of worship in the city of David.

On each of these important occasions, leaders provided instrumental music and sang their praise to God. As the temple foundation was laid under Ezra's direction, 'They sang responsively, praising and giving thanks to the Lord, saying, For he is good, for his mercy and loving-kindness endure for ever toward Israel' (Ezra 3:11, *AB*).

At the dedication in David's time they sang: 'Give thanks to the LORD, for he is good; his love endures for ever' (1 Chronicles 16:34). At the dedication in Solomon's day: 'Accompanied by trumpets, cymbals and other instruments, they raised their voices in praise to the LORD and sang: "He is good; his love endures for ever" ' (2 Chronicles 5:13).

Each of these momentous occasions made a lasting impression on the consciousness of the people of Israel. David blessed the people in God's name and gave them food to take home. After Solomon's prayer the temple was filled with the glory of the Lord, the people celebrated for many days and then went home overjoyed. At Ezra's stone-laying, people shouted and wept for joy.

Psalm 136 is a Sabbath morning psalm still recited in synagogue services. How often could we insert the timeless affirmation, 'His love endures for ever' in our Christian worship today?

Beyond Comprehension

'He said to them, "The Son of Man is going to be betrayed into the hands of men. They will kill him, and after three days he will rise"' (v. 31).

Besides Moses, the three disciples also saw Elijah on the mount of transfiguration. On the descent, when Jesus mentioned his resurrection, it was Elijah's appearance that stirred related questions. Jews knew that in preparation for the Messiah, a new Elijah would come to get the nation ready. The disciples may have thought that such a national spiritual renewal could prevent the Messiah from having to suffer.

Jesus made it clear that the forerunner's coming would not negate the Son of Man's suffering. He also said that the Elijah had already come. Mark shows that Jesus identified John the Baptist as the Elijah figure even though John had not recognised his own true significance. Earlier when people asked John, '"Then who are you? Are you Elijah?" He said, "I am not." "Are you the Prophet?" He answered, "No"' (John 1:21).

On the walk down the mountain when Jesus said that 'they have done to him everything they wished' (v. 13), he was talking about the cruel death Herod and Herodias decreed for John. Elijah the prophet also suffered at the hands of a spiteful royal couple – Ahab and Jezebel.

What their opponents did to Elijah and John, men and women unreceptive to God's message would do to Christ. Jesus connected John's mistreatment and demise with his own.

At the foot of the mountain, crowds waited for Jesus' return, wanting his help. When Jesus was again alone with his disciples in Galilee he plainly told them of his coming betrayal, death and resurrection. Not even Peter argued with him this time.

Although Jesus pointed toward the victory of resurrection, Mark says they were afraid to ask what he meant. Matthew says Jesus' followers were grief-stricken. Eventually they would personally embrace his sacrificial love and triumph over sin and death, but not yet.

To pray:

Father, help me to continue to pray for people I know who have not yet personally embraced your expansive love.

Seeing Jesus' Way

'He replied, "This kind can come out only by prayer"' (v. 29).

The three dazzled disciples who had the transforming experience and rare time alone with Jesus know he told them to keep what happened confidential but may think they can recount their encounter privately when they rejoin the other nine at the base of the mountain. As usual, a crowd interposes. When Moses returned from his lengthy mountain-top stay, in their impatience the crowd of Israelites at the base of Sinai had devolved into idol worship. Jesus had been gone only overnight. Yet the throng is so involved in their circumstances and the disciples' dispute with the experts in Jewish law that they are surprised to see Jesus. When they see him they run to him *immediately*.

Jesus has been thinking about the coming crisis of the cross, but that does not keep him from being sensitive to the daily needs of others. He came for the world, yet could see the individual. He gave himself fully to each person who came to him. As usual, Jesus arrives at the right moment and asks an insightful question.

The epileptic's father gives the details of his son's plight and the disciples' inability to help. Jesus' response reveals his despair at his followers' ineffectiveness. Does he wonder how the gospel would ever be spread when he was gone? He can't deal with that at the moment, but he can handle the issue at hand. He can help the boy, so he calls for him. The boy's grand mal seizure speaks for itself. Jesus gives the father the terms of his son's deliverance – the father's belief that it is possible.

The man came looking for Jesus but had been discouraged by the disciples, so when he does encounter Christ it is with a cautious, 'if you can do anything'. But Jesus inspires his faith and Mark says he *immediately* responds, 'I believe. Help me with my doubts!' (v. 24, *MSG*). People may disappoint us, but when we approach Jesus himself, our faith is renewed. Jesus rid the boy of his malady and lifted him to his feet and to new possibilities.

To pray:

Lord, help me to trust you, to stay in tune with you, and stay alert to opportunities to be your instrument today.

Dying to Serve

'If anyone wants to be first, he must be the very last, and the servant of all' (v. 35).

Now that time is short and Jesus still has much to cover with his disciples they leave northern Galilee and start south, ultimately for Jerusalem. Jesus seeks precious private time with them in Capernaum. As usual, Mark gives us only the essential outline of the lessons Jesus taught in his discipleship briefing.

On the way, Jesus tells the disciples that the Son of Man will be delivered into the hands of men and killed. Matthew and Luke record this as well. Mark and Matthew add that Jesus assures his followers that he will rise again. Evil will not permanently triumph. This should have eased the sting, or at least piqued their interest.

Perhaps they have selective hearing or can't comprehend what Jesus says. What they do hear seems to dash their hopes. Luke says they don't understand and are afraid to ask about it. When we receive a devastating diagnosis from the doctor, we may be numb or unable to bring ourselves to ask about treatments or prognosis. Matthew recalls that they were filled with grief.

Grief, fear and other extreme stresses generate various responses, coping strategies and behaviour. Some people withdraw or become silent while others become hyperactive or loquacious. The disciples' reaction to Jesus' disturbing declaration turns into an argument on another topic – which of them is greatest. Perhaps they wonder why Jesus chose only three of them to go up the mountain.

Jesus doesn't interrupt but is aware of their dispute. When he challenges them about it they fall silent. Mark tells us that Jesus is seated in the house – the position a rabbi takes when instructing his students – when he addresses the nub of their quarrel.

Greatness in God's kingdom comes from choosing to serve others. The question is not how I can advance in others' eyes but how I can advance God's purposes in God's way. In a society that idealised adult men, to show kindness to a child symbolised helping the least. Jesus holds a child – perhaps Peter's – as he says that welcoming the least is welcoming the Father and the Son. Giving such dignity to service is radical. Jesus himself is its best illustration (Philippians 2:6–8).

Primer on Prejudice

'For whoever is not against us is for us' (v. 40).

While in college, one of the electives courses I chose was Racial and Ethnic Minorities. In addition to contemporary works, we read the classic *The Nature of Prejudice* by Gordon W. Allport. The writer used the definition of prejudice: 'a feeling, favourable or unfavourable, toward a person or thing, prior to, or not based on, actual experience'. Bias may be pro or con, but usually bias about people unlike us is negative.

Something Jesus says prompts John to announce what he and other disciples did to defend keeping Jesus' band of followers exclusive. They'd seen someone they didn't know working in Jesus' name and had stopped him. Not only was he unauthorised, but apparently was successful in casting out demons – contrary to the disciples' recent experience with the epileptic boy.

John must have expected the Master's commendation for protecting his reputation and mission. Instead, Jesus broadens the circle and says they should allow that people doing good things in his name are not opposed to him or the mission of the gospel. They should be glad that God is blessing others as well. There is room for wide diversity in God's kingdom.

Jesus goes further. 'Why, anyone by just giving you a cup of water in my name is on our side. Count on it that God will notice' (v. 41, *MSG*). Conversely, people who stand in the way of the faith of others – especially of the most helpless – won't know God's blessing. It is a serious thing intentionally to cause another person to lose spiritual light, to turn someone aside from following Christ or to enable them to sin.

Jesus sternly condemns it – says drowning would be better than the judgement such behaviour will incur. We can easily point to elements in society that would blatantly or subtly steer us that way. But Jesus usually speaks to us individually.

What about our choices and attitudes? Perhaps we need to ask the Holy Spirit to sensitise us so that our actions and words that affect others are less critical, faith-crushing or sectarian and more encouraging, uplifting and welcoming in the spirit of Jesus. Anyone for a drink of cool water?

Serious Discipleship

'If your hand causes you to sin, cut it off. It is better for you to enter life maimed than with two hands to go into hell, where the fire never goes out' (v. 43).

Jesus tells us that occasions of stumbling will certainly come. Some may come from without, as mentioned in verse 42, but others may come from within ourselves. Jesus warns of a bleak future for the unrepentant whose deliberate actions determine a course into hell.

We hear news reports of some who have saved their lives by amputating one of their limbs with whatever was at hand, such as a penknife. They usually have been trapped in deserted places and without hope of rescue. Jesus doesn't call for literal dismemberment. Removing a thieving hand doesn't change a dishonest heart.

Today, sacrificing the use of a mobile phone, the internet or television may seem as extreme as cutting off one's hand. We depend on them. But if we can identify them as things that present irresistible temptation and take us a step closer to enabling sin in our lives, they may need to be relinquished for a time.

Jesus' stern warning means that worthwhile life goals entail sacrifice. Commonplace things, however normally useful, may need to be surrendered. Jesus urges prompt and decisive action toward whatever compromises our spiritual health or life.

In verses 45 and 47, description of divine judgement is 'thrown into hell', but in verse 43 it is the individual who chooses (literally) 'to go into hell, where the fire never goes out' through his actions. It's both the natural result of personal decision and divine verdict.

In some manuscripts, perhaps for emphasis, verse 48 is also included in verses 44 and 46. The quotation from Isaiah 66:24 stands in stark contrast to the rest of Isaiah's hopeful closing chapter about the triumph of God's kingdom and its blessings for those who obey his word. As the last verse of the book of Isaiah, it describes the eternal torment of those who rebel against God. Likewise Jesus' serious message points to the importance of turning to the Holy One of Israel.

Salted with the Spirit's Fire

'Have salt in yourselves, and be at peace with each other' (v. 50).

Although not commonly used together as an expression, salt and fire do have connections in Scripture, especially when involving sacrifice. Wycliffe's version of verse 49 clearly links salt and fire with sacrifice: 'Every man shall be salted with fire, and every slain sacrifice shall be made savoury with salt.'

What could Jesus mean? Adam Clarke suggests that the allusion could be to the cleansing of metal articles – such as in Numbers 31:22, 23 when the gold, silver, bronze, iron, tin or lead booty Israel's soldiers brought back from battle needed to be purified by fire and water.

'Everyone will be salted with fire' could mean that all human beings experience fiery experiences and whether they are of a refining or consuming nature depends on each person's relationship with God.

It could also be that Jesus was especially preparing the disciples for coming trials that would sear them as utterly as a bolt of lightning (one of the meanings of the Greek word used here for fire).

At Pentecost, after Jesus' death, resurrection and ascension, these disciples would see what looked like fire resting on the believers who had prayed and waited for the promised Holy Spirit. The flames portrayed the presence of God, reminiscent of times he had represented himself by fire in the Old Testament.

Salt is thought not to be destroyed by fire and reminds us of the salt used with sacrificial offerings for the altar. It symbolised Israel's imperishable covenant relationship with God (Leviticus 2:13). Perhaps Jesus was recalling that those who turn to the Lord are represented as his offering (Isaiah 66:20).

When followers of Christ are salted by the Holy Spirit, he suffuses us and we become something more savoury than we were. The fire represents the holiness of God and the eternal flame of his love. When the Spirit salts us with fire, he purifies, establishes, influences and preserves us – marinates us, as it were – thereby helping us to be more than we ever thought we could be.

Jesus called his disciples to that plane of living which would result in enjoying peace with each other. He calls us to it as well.

God is Enough

'Your name, O Lord, endures forever, your renown, O Lord, through all generations' (v. 13).

Today's psalm has been called a mosaic of three Old Testament sections – the law, the prophets and the psalms. Some of its verses are similar to those of other psalms, especially Psalm 115, one of the set of *Hallel* songs which was used during festivals. Today's song praises the Lord's greatness and faithfulness.

Its opening call to the servants of the Lord who stand in his house might build on Psalm 134 since it, too, is initially addressed to them. But the injunctions aren't restricted to the clergy or liturgical singers. We are all expected to praise the Lord because he is good and to sing praise to his name because 'it is pleasant' (v. 3, *KJV*). Is it singing praise to his name, or his name itself that the psalmist means is pleasant? Translations differ. Perhaps it can be both.

Do we need particular reasons to praise the Lord? The psalmist cites three: God's love which chose a people through whom to bless all nations, his creative power and his sovereignty. They are all demonstrated throughout the tapestry of history. He gives illustrations of each.

We can do the same with our personal histories. We can witness to knowing God's great love proven in our lives. We can recall being in awe of something he has created, whether as grand as the northern or southern lights or as minuscule as star sand (star-shaped exoskeletons of marine protozoa found on certain Pacific Ocean beaches). We can affirm that God who is good is in charge of our present and future and will exonerate his followers and have compassion on us (v. 14).

As we worship God on this Lord's Day we can continue to trust him and his sufficiency. We can sing with Salvationist songwriter Herbert Howard Booth the threefold affirmation, 'I will trust thee, I will trust thee, I will trust thee, all my life thou shalt control' (*SASB* 713). And we can say what the writer of Psalm 135 said from its start and at its finish – a heartfelt 'Praise the Lord!'

Love at Home

'Let no one split apart what God has joined together' (v. 9).

Whereas in Mark 9 Jesus taught his disciples privately, at the outset of Mark 10 God's Servant–Son enlarges his teaching circle. He leaves Galilee for the last time before the crucifixion. He moves resolutely toward Jerusalem. Jesus takes a circuitous route, walking south through the Jordan valley into Judea, then east across the Jordan to the hill country of Perea.

Mark records only some of the final events during Jesus' time in the region. As people swarm around him he's in public ministry again. As usual, as he teaches, Jewish leaders try to entrap him with calculated questions to prove him heretical.

Pharisees hope to embroil him either with Herod Antipas, who was censured by John the Baptist for marrying his brother's wife, or with the Sanhedrin through conflict with the law. Perhaps they think Jesus will contradict his earlier teaching. Jesus replies to their ploy with a different question: 'What did Moses command you?' (v. 3).

They summarise verses from Deuteronomy 24 to imply that when Moses permitted a man to divorce a woman 'because he finds something indecent about her' (v. 1), it could be for any of a wide variety of reasons that irritated him. They conveniently hold Mosaic concession as licence. In Jesus' day, because divorce commonly occurred for trivial reasons, women hesitated to marry.

The way Jesus responds shows his concern for marriage and for women. The basic attitude of the day was based on an assumption that women were less than men, and could even be viewed as things rather than with the dignity of persons.

The authority Jesus quotes goes back further than the law of Moses – to the Genesis creation story and God's original design. He stands against casual attitudes about human beings and about divinely initiated institutions. Marriage carries responsibility as well as opportunity for spiritual unity. William Barclay says: 'Jesus was building a rampart around the home.'[2]

To pray:

Lord, help us to show that we value each other and honour you in our homes.

Blessing the Defenceless

'And He took [the children up one by one] in His arms and [fervently invoked a] blessing, placing His hands upon them' (v. 16, AB).

During June each year, a global network of organisations draws attention to children at risk and asks for concentrated prayer for them. Hundreds of millions of children are exploited as child labourers or soldiers. UNICEF says that more than one billion children suffer from extreme deprivation. Our prayers and gifts are especially important to these most vulnerable people in our world.

As in Matthew's Gospel, children enter the scene with Jesus right after his teaching on marriage. If women weren't considered important, in some ways neither were children. Jesus corrects that. No doubt the scene was repeated often throughout Christ's ministry. Luke tells us that infants were brought to Jesus.

In some lands, parents plant a tree when a child is born. There are particular customs to recognise children's birthdays especially in places where infant mortality is high. Besides the obligatory dedication of a newborn with appropriate offerings in thanks to God, it was Jewish custom for parents to have a distinguished rabbi bless their children on their first birthdays. Although some of the children brought to Jesus in today's Scripture may have been celebrating their birthdays, the word Mark uses for children can include babies to pre-teens – as might attend a church family picnic.

We may be surprised to think of Jesus attracting children, especially as he faced his approaching death. Jesus could have been preoccupied with the weight of knowing he was on his way to the cross. Mark says that on this occasion the parents kept on bringing the children and the disciples kept on rebuking them. Possibly Jesus' followers were trying to protect him, but their reproof of the parents pained Jesus. Jesus made time for children. Perhaps the children's receptive spirits were a blessing to him.

Only Mark tells us that Jesus took the children in his arms, cradled them, put his hands on them and fervently blessed them. Even if we now have wrinkled faces, we can imagine ourselves as children in that scene and look into the kind face of Jesus today. Let's also determine to bring blessing to the lives of children.

A Man Who Wouldn't

'Go, sell everything you have and give to the poor, and you will have treasure in heaven. Then come, follow me' (v. 21).

After Jesus reminded listeners that receiving God's gift of eternal life must be in childlike trust, he encountered a man who wouldn't operate that way. Mark says he ran up to Jesus and knelt in front of him to ask his question respectfully. His approach, posture and form of address showed his eagerness, sincerity and respect for Jesus' spiritual teaching. Yet his question belied his quest. He said he sought eternal life and wanted to know what he could do to achieve it.

When Jesus challenged the way he addressed him as good (v. 18) he wasn't lessening his divinity or purity, he was making a veiled claim to it, and also subtly correcting the then common rabbinic adage: 'There is nothing that is good but the law.'

Jesus told him he already knew what this good God required. He reviewed five of the Ten Commandments which dealt with human relationships and so could be borne out in a person's conduct. He then added something applicable to the wealthy: 'do not defraud', which complemented the commandments about not stealing, giving false testimony or dishonouring one's parents. In that day, people sometimes used a loophole to theoretically tie their assets to the temple so they wouldn't have to support their parents, and so could protect their wealth.

The seeker after truth said he'd kept these commandments from his youth (bar mitzvah age). In effect he said he'd never harmed anyone. Perhaps that was true, but with all he had, what had he sacrificially done for anyone? Jesus lovingly peered into the young man's soul, which was self- and wealth-possessed, and offered him a radical opportunity to live up to his potential. The young man responded by choosing his possessions over treasure in heaven. No wonder he left with a gloomy countenance, although some believe he later reconsidered and became the follower named Barnabas.[3]

It's a question not of what we haven't done, but of whether we've given ourselves selflessly for Christ and others. Following Jesus in love for and obedience to God, not achievement or respectability, leads to goodness and eternal life.

Reversals

'How hard it is for those who trust in riches to enter the kingdom of God!' (v. 24, NKJV).

The seeker who arrived in high spirits and perhaps out of breath leaves low-spirited under the cloud of his refusal to follow Jesus' direction. Jesus turns back to his disciples and comments that it's difficult for those with riches to enter God's kingdom. The disciples can't believe he would say such a thing. Once again their Master challenges popular belief. Their cultural mindset was that prosperity was an indication of goodness and blessing.

For clarity Jesus repeats himself and amplifies that those who *trust* in riches have trouble entering the kingdom. He uses a well-known hyperbole about the camel and needle for emphasis. We can imagine the dumbfounded disciples shrugging their shoulders in resignation when they say to each other: 'Who then can be saved?' (v. 26).

If a person's main interests are tied to possessions, they primarily think about their cost rather than true value. Riches can easily affect attitudes about oneself and others. How people obtain wealth interests us, but equally important is how they use it. Today, when every pendulum swing of economic news strikes fear in individuals, institutions and nations, Jesus' counsel about misplaced trust in assets remains relevant.

The disciples conclude that if the most advantaged can't enter God's kingdom, then ordinary people have no chance. Humanly speaking they are right. Jesus reminds them that even things that appear impossible with people are possible with God. Eternal life is not a lifetime achievement award, but a gift of God who offers it to everyone who will receive it. The entrance fee is the same for all.

Peter doesn't consider the rich man's loss as much as what he and the disciples would gain by the sacrifices they'd made to follow Christ. Jesus assures them that whatever they've given up for his sake would be repaid.

To set aside thoughts of quid pro quo reward for sacrifice, he adds that they would also know persecution, gain eternal life and find their notions of first and last reversed. What a colossal concept to consider – for all of us!

The Servant of the Lord

'For even the Son of Man did not come to be served, but to serve, and to give his life as a ransom for many' (v. 45).

Mark's narrative gains momentum as he describes Jesus' next steps. Now, after time in the northern mountains, near the Sea of Galilee, then in the hill country to the south, he is literally going up to Jerusalem, which is more than 2,500 feet above sea level. The physical exertion required to walk there suggests strains on other levels. Yet Jesus strides out ahead of his followers as their courageous leader. His resolve amazes the disciples. Others are fearful, probably for their own safety. We wonder what exit options they consider.

Again Jesus frankly tells his band of men details of his impending death. His declaration this time is the fullest of the three that Mark records. For the first time Jesus mentions the Gentiles' participation in it. He uses specific verbs: 'The Son of Man will be *betrayed* to the chief priests and teachers of the law. They will *condemn* him to death and will *hand him over* to the Gentiles, who will *mock* him and *spit on* him, *flog* him and *kill* him. Three days later he will *rise*' (vv. 33, 34).

The disciples should begin to grasp the gravity of it all. Yet they are clueless and in juxtaposition to Jesus' serious declaration, some scheme for position. James and John may feel entitled to do so, either as part of the inner circle or because they come from a well-off family. It seems they may want to outshine Peter and share Christ's authority, since that's what sitting on his right and left hand implies. At least they are hopeful that eventually Jesus will triumph and there will actually be a kingdom.

Jesus takes their foolish request seriously and asks if they can endure what he faces. Brashly they say they can. Ultimately both did experience some of the cup and baptism of Christ's suffering. James was the first martyred apostle (Acts 12:2) and John was persecuted and exiled (Revelation 1:9).

Although their insensitivity must hurt Jesus and stir up the others, he patiently points out the nature of the kingdom as he reminds them, and us, of the high calling of sacrificial service.

Hidden in Plain Sight

'"What do you want me to do for you?" Jesus asked him' (v. 51).

As Jesus proceeds toward Jerusalem his route passes through Jericho. In conjunction with his winter residence, Herod the Great built this city about fifteen miles from Jerusalem in the vicinity of the Jericho of Old Testament fame. It lay within the radius of Jerusalem within which Jewish males over the age of twelve were required to attend Passover. Also, due to Jericho's proximity to the temple, thousands of off-duty priests and temple attendants stayed there as they awaited their turn for religious service. No wonder verse 46 says there was a large crowd going out of Jericho that day.

Jesus' act of mercy for a beggar is the final recorded healing miracle in Mark's Gospel. It comes at the end of Jesus' course of intensive instruction for the disciples. Soon after Jesus defuses the indignation of the ten at the presumptuous request of the two, he encounters another request. We notice the contrast between the outlook of the recently ambitious disciples and the focus of the blind man. While the sighted pair spun notions of future power, the blind one knows his current need is for sight. Perhaps Jesus hopes this encounter will instruct his followers about spiritual insight.

Only Mark gives us the man's name – Bartimaeus, or Timaeus's son. He must be a persistent, hopeful man since he shouts above the din of the crowd and the censure of many. Jesus notices and stops to speak to this one individual. Perhaps he now tells the very ones who were trying to silence the man to call him. 'It's all right now,' they tell him (v. 49, *JBP*). Bartimaeus is ready.

As Jesus had said to his ambitious disciples, he says to Bartimaeus, 'What do you want me to do for you?' and gives opportunity to verbalise a particular need. He gives us the same opportunity as we approach him.

Earlier the man called out to Jesus, Son of David. Now he uses an affectionate term of reverence and respect as he calls him what Mary did on the first Easter, *Rabboni* (my teacher, master), and simply says, 'I want to see.' Jesus pronounces him healed. Now sighted, he gratefully and loyally follows Jesus. Is that our response?

A People's Songbook

'Praise the LORD, all you servants of the LORD' (v. 1).

Certain psalms fall into distinct groups. Perhaps the most obvious are the fifteen psalms from 120 to 134 which comprise a people's songbook. Each is titled 'a song of degrees', 'a song of ascents' or 'a pilgrim song'. Commentators differ about the titles' meaning. Some think they refer to the tunes used or the high pitch at which they were sung. Others suppose they are a reference to climbing the steps to the temple.

J. Sidlow Baxter believes the reference is to the degrees on the royal sundial in the days of godly Hezekiah, king of Judah. When he was ill and heard God's message through Isaiah to prepare to die, Hezekiah prayed that his life would be spared. God answered the king's prayer and promised that the king would be well enough to worship at the temple in three days. God also granted him fifteen more years of life. When the king requested a sign of this promise, God temporarily turned back the royal clock (sun's shadow). Since Hezekiah was the author of several songs, some of this set may have been written by him in gratitude for extra years of life.

Although the songs might have been used when the people returned from the Babylonian captivity, most scholars hold that these fifteen psalms, comprised of 101 verses, were sung by pilgrims en route to the annual festivals held in Jerusalem. Since the city is on a hill, people would literally go up to Jerusalem.

Today's brief psalm is certainly similar to the opening of Psalm 135 as it addresses God's servants who stand in his house. In Psalm 134, those voicing verses 1 and 2 seek to support those on sacred service which continues even through the night. In verse 3 we hear a response from those who receive this encouragement to continue their important ministry. As if in confirmation that, yes, they will go on with it, they reply with a special blessing on their encouragers.

It is reminiscent of the benediction from the Lord which the priests used to bless the people: 'The LORD bless you and keep you; the LORD make his face shine upon you and be gracious to you; the LORD turn his face towards you and give you peace' (Numbers 6:24–26). It remains an excellent gift to receive and pass on today.

Social Justice

A look at God's word of creation, liberation and transformation

Introduction

The writings during the next four weeks are from the pen of Commissioner M. Christine MacMillan, the first Director of The Salvation Army's International Social Justice Commission (ISJC). The mandate of the ISJC is to advise The Salvation Army on social, economic and political issues and events. The ISJC team exerts a significant influence for good at the United Nations. The Secretariat is based in New York City, ten blocks from the United Nations.

The commissioner's devotional comments will help us understand justice from a biblical perspective (using the *New Living Translation*[4] throughout) with our feet planted in human experience. Since she frequently uses verses from the same passage of Scripture, when there are repeats we suggest reading them in different versions.

Commissioner MacMillan, a Canadian, has lived and worked in five countries, experiencing widely different culture, values, faith and approaches to life as, for thirty-five years, she has lived out her mission as a Salvation Army officer. As well as serving in the UK and Australia, she has been Territorial Commander for Papua New Guinea and more recently the Canada and Bermuda Territory. She is committed to ministry in the belief that a redemptive capacity must be the influential thread through all social justice activities and thinking.

God's Dream in Creation

'In the beginning God created the heavens and the earth' (v. 1).

When you woke up this morning what ideas stirred your imagination? Looking at the first recorded words of Scripture provides not just facts but ideas leading to creative action. When The Salvation Army first put its feet on God's Earth it was as if a sleeping Church rolled out of bed. This new Christian movement became alive as a God-creation from heaven flowing through earth like an ever-flowing river of justice and righteousness (see Amos 5:24).

My early beginnings of ministry took on new ideas when The Salvation Army was successful in submitting a bid to operate a secure, anonymous shelter for battered women and children. Subsequently a succession of broken dreams walked through the front door of our Kate Booth House.

Picture the day a woman and child entered, holding onto each other for dear life. The little one was brought to mingle with similar victims in the children's play area. Her mom found herself at our dining-room table after many days of being treated abusively and deprived of food. She presented herself from the neck up with a face swollen, black and blue – not unlike a punchbag – where hands of monstrous injustice had gone to work.

A curious young child resident at the home plonked herself at the table directly across from the newcomer. Our worker stared in her direction with eyes that read, 'Don't you dare pass comment!' Our curiosity-seeker, unable to hold back, opened her little mouth with words only heaven could send: 'Oh, what beautiful hair you have!' In that moment, heaven and earth kissed – lighting up that room with massive love. The bruised and swollen face, so long wreathed in darkness, broke into a smile.

Imagine

As you begin your day, what heaven and earth kisses can you contribute to an unjust world?

God's Dream in the Darkness

'The earth was formless and empty, and darkness covered the deep waters' (v. 2).

Today I think of the swollen stomachs of the 30,000 children who die unfed every day. What a darkness of death! At least the awareness of such a dreadful situation is the beginning of change. The drama of Jesus' death also encompasses darkness: 'At noon darkness fell across the whole land until three o'clock' (Mark 15:33). This darkness has a voice, as Jesus in death cries, 'My God, my God, why have you forsaken me?'

I recall, as a young girl, waking up unexpectedly in hospital and my mother standing by my bed with her winter coat on over her nightgown. What was happening? I had suddenly been taken seriously ill and my mother had had no time for preparation before accompanying her unconscious daughter in the ambulance.

Upon rousing in a strange setting, I asked my mother if I was having my tonsils out. Obviously my thinking was askew, as my tonsils had been removed a few years earlier. I was in the dark. I tried to move my body and suddenly felt intense pain. The illness was now informing me about the darkness. When life dishes up meaninglessness, who will check out the pain?

Coping with the pain of injustice doesn't come easily or naturally. It poses so many questions. For me that little girl incident taught me that pain and darkness often accompany each other. For the next few weeks after that incident I placed my pain in the hands of medical staff who nursed my body back to health.

Too many unnecessary deaths take place every day because resources are unequally shared throughout the world.

Let's face it

Explore the darkness with a courage that looks as if it rushed to get there.

God's Dream Emerges

'And the Spirit of God was hovering over the surface' (v. 3).

Decision-making often causes tension through the dilemma of options. We ponder the various possibilities, but weighing up risks, seeking assurances, counting the cost and trying to be wise and prudent can be faith-limiting.

The Spirit of God is mysterious and threatening to our natural unwillingness to live without ambiguity. Yet when we sing about the Spirit, alluding to his motivation behind our decision-making, we say we long for his creative force of empowerment. At creation, God's Spirit, interpreted as wind or breath, filled God's lungs to perform an epic-making extravaganza which humankind subsequently explored for centuries.

The result, which we call Earth, and which we also call home, is a visual, physical outcome of this hovering creative energy of God. Now, eons later, God's Spirit still hovers over his creation and he is breathless still, as there is still more to give. The Spirit of God waits patiently and listens for our invitation: 'Spirit of the living God, fall afresh on me . . . Break me, mould me, fill me, use me.' (*SASB* chorus 53)

Invited, God enters with his creative breath of life, and we understand the glorious unending possibilities of his creative power. 'Long ago ever before he made the world, God loved us' (Ephesians 1:4).

Dream

I dream of a day not far, far away,
When in the world of men the love of God shall be seen.
(John Gowans in the Salvation Army musical, Take-Over Bid*)*

God's Dream Ignites

'Then God said, "Let there be light", and there was light' (Genesis 1:3).

A few blocks from where I live in New York is the expanse of Central Park, an oasis of activity that brings opportunity for reflection and refreshment to skyscraper-enclosed city-dwellers. Tucked in among a clump of fenced greenery is one particular place I love to visit. This oval-shaped enclosure with a few park benches faces inward to a memorial at ground level. The focus of attention is a one-word inscription: 'Imagine'. People come here from all corners of the earth, many to sing the songs of their lost hero, singer and songwriter John Lennon, gunned down outside his apartment a mere stone's throw from here. While some sing, others sit quietly, in grief or quiet contemplation.

Our creation story also now sits in audio mode. The formless mass cloaked in darkness is about to hear the alarm bell go off. Shades drawn will now be lifted as the Creator God in authority speaks: 'Let there be light.'

Growing up in an era of Beatle-mania, one sensed a revival in the message music of those four British pop stars. They emerged on the world's stage with songs about love, particularly in the words of a John Lennon song which spoke of a dream for the world to become one. Spiritual dimensions were often phrased as lyrics and sung outside the orbit of stained-glass windows. Their famous song, 'Let it be', etched its way into the souls of countless seekers who echoed the next phrase: 'There will be an answer, let it be.'

God's dictum, 'Let there be light', finds an answer and there is light. Our response can result in more light – or we can reply with cloaked whispers of veiled criticism which extinguish light.

Injustice has many root-word sources but the simplest description goes something like this: acts and attitudes of subversive darkness shut down voices whose challenges would shed light.

Let it be

Turning your face to God, listen for his voice as you become the answer through mirrored reflection.

God's Dream Enlightens

'And God saw that the light was good. Then he separated the light from the darkness' (v. 4).

In my role as Director of The Salvation Army's International Social Justice Commission (ISJC), figuring out light from darkness is a constant duty. The halls of the United Nations see The Salvation Army's uniformed presence. Our desire as an ISJC team is to make an authentic contribution. To this end, we have become familiar with the Millennium Development Goals as a focus of our research, teaching, policy and coalition-building work.

These goals have become the conviction of nations, outliving any other project of a unified nature in history. Issues such as gender equality, accessible education for children, maternal health care and sustainable development are separating out the darkness of marginalisation into the light of hope.

The creation story relates stated goals which by God's intervention are realised. I try to picture God's lab-coat techniques in separating darkness from light and realise I am not a scientist. However, I am one who wants to understand differences and make a difference. I spend much time in separating out the Jesus way from my way.

I have often told the story of a fired-up church group who on a Sunday morning moved from their urban setting to preach the gospel to a skid row audience, where I spent fourteen years in ministry, usually in the evening hours. The microphoned evangelists saw the scraggly few before them as deaf to God's awareness. At one juncture, my park bench friends turned to us as we walked by. Looking over to the pulpit preachers, then back to us, they commented, 'Why are they yelling at us? We *know* we are sinners!'

Separation in God's eyes is not relegated to 'us and them'. Rather, it separates the injustice of behaviour that views sin as a challenge that confronts us all.

Development goals

Bring before God those prejudicial attitudes which prevent issues being seen clearly in the light of day.

God's Dream and Us

'So God created human beings in his own image. In the image of God he created them; male and female he created them' (v. 27).

In their book, *Renovation of the Heart in Daily Practice*, Dallas Willard and Jan Johnson state: 'Two of the most powerful facets in the realm of human thought are ideas and images. Ideas are ways of thinking, and images the concrete expression of our ideas.'[5] God's dreams and ideas looked for a pattern that recreated Earth's vastness into a single image.

The word in God's ideal shows up in Jesus. In the book of Genesis and in the Gospel of John we compare a similar pattern of recording. Both books start with 'In the beginning'. In Genesis 1:27 we are orbited into a fresh humility that God would create us in his image. This begins to stretch our imagination. Jumping to John 1:1, the beginning refers to a word idea becoming an image of life.

From the beginning, The Salvation Army's mission has been marked with love for God, service among the poor and the invitation to believe and follow Jesus Christ. The challenge is to harmonise creation and historic mission with God's call to pursue justice in today's world.

Believing from Genesis 1:27 that everyone is created in the image of God, we struggle with the different outcomes. We lament the abusive and unethical behaviour imposed on vulnerable people.

We want to know God in more than mere symbol, driven by informed conviction and ideas, lived out in creative compassion, with a justice that challenges human inequity and reaches out from the intelligence of the heart.

Individuals full of ideas are dreamers of sorts. The God dreamer communicates with his creation. His soil becomes inhabited by male and female footprints of significant imprint. 'The Word gave life to everything that was created, and his life brought light to everyone' (John 1:4).

A child's idea of God sings: 'God's not dead, he is alive!' A dreaming adult child of God sings: 'Breathe on me, breath of God, fill me with life anew.'

Call to Unity

'And we all hear these people speaking in our own languages about the wonderful things God has done!' (v. 11).

Christians around the world meet on this day of Pentecost far more spread out than that initial gathering of the Holy Spirit's explosive visitation. Language is both frustrating and comforting. If the words are foreign to your ear, you tune out the babble. Conversing in your own language is exhilarating and falls into a natural pattern of communication.

At one time the whole world spoke a single language, as Genesis 11 states, and isolation was the result. The one-language people plotted to build a tower to keep them from scattering all over the world.

> When the most high came down and confused the tongues, he divided the nations; but when he distributed the tongues of fire, he called all to unity. Therefore with one voice, we glorify the all-Holy Spirit! (Orthodox Kontakion of the Feast of Pentecost)

The one-language society also had a visitation – the Lord came and said: 'If they can accomplish this when they have just begun to take advantage of their common language and political unity, just think what they will do later. Come, let's go down and give them different languages. Then they won't be able to understand each other.'

The miracle of Pentecost speaks of differences being celebrated in the unity of exchanging language for language as the Holy Spirit enabled everyone to understand what was said as if it was in their own tongue (Acts 2:4, 11b).

There is so much in our world we don't understand (including ourselves, sometimes). Thinking globally knocks down towers of assuming 'our world' is right and needs to be protected from the different views of others.

Sing

Release your Spirit song today out of the cages of prejudice into a God-so-loved world.

God's Prophetic Liberation

'Listen to me, my people. Hear me . . . for my law will be proclaimed and my justice will become a light to the nations' (v. 4).

The art of listening is a prerequisite for the counselling room. Taking this a step further we begin to hear. Listening and hearing intentionally become discovery trails into the unknown. This week we will listen in to Isaiah's faithful insights of a God who longs for his prophetic liberation. Scripture in the prophetic realm of social justice is not a take-it-or-leave-it proclamation. The volume is turned up and the atmosphere is heated. God's heart is breaking.

One discovers through the wail of outcries that justice is not merely an attribute of God, a thrown-in extra or a personality trait. Far from it, justice is the essence of who God is – the core of his being. God wants to get our attention in the comfort of sharing formidable news in the intimacy of our living room. Strong messages can reap fearful responses. The very way he names himself is daunting: 'Lord Almighty'!

As a delegate at The Salvation Army's International College for Officers, my world view was given new horizons. Coming to the end of our time together we started the round of goodbyes. In conversation, Anna invited me to her African country to meet her husband, children and people. 'You come to my country,' she said. Looking into my eyes, to assure me of a warm welcome, she said: 'I will tell them you are mine.'

Tucked away in the midst of the prophetic demands of Isaiah 51 there is a by-the-way insert of this God 'who stirs up the sea, causing its waves to roar' (v. 14). He desires to set a foundation of relationship and acceptance. 'And I have put my words in your mouth and have hidden you safely in my hand. I stretched out the sky like a canopy and laid the foundations of the earth. I am the one who says . . . "You are my people!" ' (Isaiah 51:16).

Holding on

Picture your life in the hands of God by listening to his words, 'You are mine' and hearing his assurance in the midst of tough messages.

Famished

' "We have fasted before you!" they say. "Why aren't you impressed? We have been very hard on ourselves, and you don't even notice it!" "I will tell you why!" I respond. "It's because you are fasting to please yourselves" ' (v. 3).

Fasting can be a helpful spiritual exercise, but not if the motivation is merely to seek God's approval or gain his attention. I wonder if telling God our spiritual achievements gets on his nerves.

How do we make sense of linking hunger and penance? Spiritual disciplines appear to require sacrifice. But reaching out to God must be more than a formula to draw the spotlight onto our piety. On the contrary, God surely wants us to look outward even while we are fasting.

We should be noticing:

- the hunger of others;
- the oppression of others;
- the imprisonment of others;
- the wandering of others;
- the helplessness of others.

As we grow up into maturity, spiritual maturity, we balance ourselves under God's discipline and discover freedom. We hear the prophet's challenge: 'Are we living for ourselves?'

Pull up your chair to God's table and see the many empty chairs – empty because people have not accepted God's invitation to be present. God is whetting our appetite and not merely our conscience. If you miss a meal do you feel hungry or guilty? If you miss a prayer do you feel hungry or guilty?

Such guilt is false guilt based on perfectionist tendencies. Sit down at the feast with God's welcome for you and those you welcome. The warmth of conversation brings community into focus.

Hunger

God feeds on possibilities of famished guests who just show up.

If Today's Children Build Tomorrow's World

'Some of you will rebuild the deserted ruins of your cities' (v. 12).

There has been considerable research into the populations around the world who are pouring each year into cities by the millions. Rural communities are becoming fewer and fewer. In one part of the world, settlements are formed from makeshift shelters of tin and cardboard. In another, the back seats of cars serve as children's beds. Too often, sidewalks are the hard mattresses for the solitary homeless.

Deserted ruins are not only abandoned buildings and farms; they are places that no longer fulfil their former roles as safe and secure homes. Children will rebuild those deserted ruins not merely by becoming architects, carpenters, plumbers and electricians. They must rebuild the world itself by tackling the causes of the inequity which led to those ruins. They will need to live counter-culturally and demonstrate God's value of loving their neighbour as themselves. That rule must be written on their hearts.

There are countries where some children live in sewers while others live in houses surrounded by well-manicured gardens. I have visited such places and I ask myself, 'If I invest my life as a mentor to the young, do I start with the gift of time?' Jesus said, 'Let the children come to me.' How wide, how deep is my response?

Ruins

Where the children are hopeful and their hands reach out, who will hold on?

Answers and Questions

'Listen! The LORD's arm is not too weak to save you, nor is his ear too deaf to hear you call' (v. 1).

The Church is a good talker, but sometimes a less good listener. It has an unhelpful habit of delivering answers without taking breath. One-way communication is like talking to a wall. The beginning of Isaiah 59 is like a shouting match. Before we allow words out of our mouth we should contemplate the matter of receptivity. Who will hear?

Picture being lost in the depths of a forest. Panic overwhelms you as you realise you have no sense of direction. Every few steps you call out: 'Is anybody there?' Your frustration escalates. Your arms tire from waving for attention, your voice is hoarse from crying out. Eventually you shut down. You become deaf to yourself. Your insignificance exhausts you. At that precise moment God's strength moves into your weakness.

Perhaps the world is saying to the Church: 'You need ears, not edicts.' The cartoonist Shultz said just this through his character Peanuts: 'Christ is the answer, but what is the question?'

Answers get formed from deep, penetrating questions, not the other way around. Weakness is turned to strength as our vulnerability looks into the unknown and waits in the silence.

Listen

If the Lord is strong to save, what needs saving?

Declarations

'Yes, truth is gone, and anyone who renounces evil is attacked. The LORD looked and was displeased to find there was no justice' (v. 15).

The need for community confession is an admission that our society has lacked compassion, justice and honesty. We have violated God by relegating his redemptive presence as a voice silenced. In 1948 the Declaration of Human Rights was signed at the United Nations as a code of conduct for civil society. I attended the sixtieth anniversary of the declaration in Paris, France, where the first signatories had declared the truths they were attesting to. The 2008 anniversary, which revisited the articles of the declaration, started with a global inventory. The 3,000 delegates explored the truthful relevance of these articles sixty years later, rediscovering standards to look up to and words of life to live by.

Sitting on the panel of one session were two conscientious objectors. In their country they saw a world needing their influence. The dictatorship of their country's president stated that assembly in the marketplace was forbidden. The next day, 139 people gathered to stand up for righteousness. All were put under arrest. While in prison, a representative of the president offered them freedom providing each signed a statement declaring they had violated the president's authority. All but two signed.

For three years the two freedom fighters sat behind bars. They were the two individuals before us. Speaking with experience on the Declaration of Human Rights, their story cried truth. Heroes willingly bear the consequences when they view the cause as greater than the applause.

Such a hero of India – Mahatma Gandhi – speaks into our conscience: 'Joy lies in the fight, in the attempt, in the suffering involved, not in the victory itself.'

Truth

When Jesus says he is truth, he is standing in the way of those who would obstruct life and justice, and he asks us to do the same.

Living Bookmarks

'The LORD has told you what is good and this is what he requires of you: to do what is right, to love mercy, and to walk humbly with your God' (v. 8).

Like Isaiah, Micah is preoccupied with social justice and with the duplicity of all leaders, political and spiritual. In Micah's messages of judgement, hope is inserted as if a new era of God's steadfast love is finding its response in a people of lamentation becoming a people of faith.

At the International Social Justice Commission we have designed bookmarks based on a familiar social justice voice of conscience – Micah 6:8. We want to respond not just out of requirement but with prophetic liberation to 'do justice, love mercy and walk humbly with our God'. The three 'justices' in everyday practice can also be looked at as:

- distributive justice – sharing resources;
- egalitarianism – walking humbly with our God;
- legislation – freedom of justice found in human rights.

Become a bookmark which lives a word picture daily as our prayers find expression in action.

Open book

Lord, may my life be your open and prophetic book with:
Inspiration to give with abandonment;
Conviction to defy injustice with passion;
Brokenness alongside victims whose hope is trampled;
Creativity to struggle with unanswered questions;
Courage to bring a shaft of light into the unknown;
Salvation to sing the songs of justice in any storm.

C. M.

Exquisite Blend

'It is good and pleasant when God's people live together in peace!' (v. 1, NCV).

The people's songbook we began to consider on Sunday 16 May, including Psalm 133, may well have been recited by the thousands who came to Jerusalem for the annual Pentecost festival. We don't know if the thought of groups of pilgrims journeying together to Jerusalem suggested the theme of today's psalm to the writer.

When a disparate group gathers around a common cause, whether in mourning or in celebration, there can be concord for a while. It's a bond we wish could last.

But verse 1 of our psalm isn't about a one-off occasion; it's about daily living. It's a notable thing when people who are related by birth, spiritual association or vocation regularly spend time together and do so in harmony. The psalmist likens such amity to two things – refreshing, necessary dew and precious oil.

Unity is like the sacred oil used for anointing the high priest. Such oil, the work of a perfumer, was a set blend of liquid myrrh, fragrant cinnamon and cane, cassia and olive oil (Exodus 30:22–25). Although each ingredient had a particular scent, together they became a new unique fragrant blend with a sacred purpose.

When, in obedience to God's command and in sight of the whole congregation of Israel, Moses poured the oil on Aaron's head, it ran down his beard and his special priestly attire (including the breastplate with the names of the twelve tribes for whom he ministered and prayed), and he was saturated. The oil symbolised a nation united for worship under their consecrated priest.

For Christians it seems natural to speak of the unity of God's people right after Pentecost Sunday. The oil serves as a metaphor for the way the Holy Spirit can blend willing believers together in love and service. Where there is unity, God pours out blessing.

To pray:

Lord, so saturate me with your Holy Spirit that I may continually please you in my relationships with others.

A Dangerous Moment

'The Spirit of the Lord is upon me because he has anointed me to . . .' (v. 18).

The local-boy-made-good returns home to Nazareth and heads off to the synagogue. The time comes for Scripture to be read and prophetic liberation is about to speak as Jesus steps forward. The unrolling of the scroll for the message of that day is not to be a case of 'shut your eyes and magically point to some words'. The unrolled Scripture had been waiting for a lifetime to have the Messiah stand to his feet and read his mission statement. The Lord's Spirit speaks good news, liberty, insight and freedom.

These are not just gracious words of Isaiah falling from the lips of Jesus of Nazareth as everyone stares at him intently, waiting for the secret to be revealed. Jesus becomes the witness to his own words: 'Then he began to speak to them. "The Scripture you've just heard has been fulfilled this very day!"' (v. 21).

The temperature rises in the synagogue and Jesus, reading their minds, suggests to the congregation that no prophet is accepted in his home town. He is right. The subject turns to dealing with differences – foreigners, you could say.

Racism raises its ugly head as the well-wishers of a few moments before become furious. The congregation becomes a lynch mob and Jesus is taken to the edge of the hill on which his home town was built. They go there not to admire the view but to throw Jesus over the cliff. But he slips away.

Mission statement

Watch out if the Spirit of the Lord comes upon you. It can be a dangerous moment!

Plant a Difference

'God blesses those who hunger and thirst for justice, for they will be satisfied' (v. 6).

If you want to get hungry and thirsty for justice, then get hungry and thirsty. The teachings of Jesus as recorded in the *be-attitudes* had him climbing a mountain to find the classroom.

As I read these attitudes of becoming, there is a part of me that is not sure of their realism. I meet a lot of spiritual appetites these days that are revolutionary in determination. But, let's face it, our digital generation has access to our world up front and it's becoming personal. Youth, our pacesetters, are hungry for change.

Every year the World Economic Forum is held in the Swiss ski resort of Davos. The *Who's Who* of social justice is there and depression can hit quickly when the talk is of recession in our world's economy.

Making the world a better place at ground level was the presentation of six teenagers who formed a panel at the forum. A youth in a shiny red jacket presented his ideas. He remembered growing up in Beijing when spring meant sandstorms choking his lungs. It was 'hell on earth'. Yunmau at age fourteen recruited people to travel to Mongolia and plant 365 trees, one for every day of the year.

Inspiration and action changes not only our behaviour but the world.

Optimism

Get off the mountain and into the sandstorm and be blessed in daring to plant a difference.

Mercy Wrap

'Now go and learn the meaning of this Scripture: I want you to show mercy, not offer sacrifices' (v. 13).

This Scripture has been a trademark of accountability since my early days of ministry. Jesus is quoting from Hosea, whose story in the Old Testament is mercy-based.

Calculated commitment robs us of ingenuity. It faces injustice with a formula of the deserving and undeserving poor. It views the obvious as whole truth and nothing but the truth. It wallows in its sacrifice as a pig in mud.

Why did Jesus use this phrase on more than one occasion: 'I desire mercy and not sacrifice'? His followers, divided into two camps, saw fans and critics who were class- and rule-conscious. One Sabbath, Jesus encouraged his hungry disciples to pick ears of corn to eat. Critics saw this as breaking a Sabbath rule. Healing on the Sabbath was also a no-no. Organisational approaches to injustice do not go far enough.

There is a Christian non-governmental global health organisation which sends medicines to needy parts of our world. The precious containers require protection – the very circumstance for which bubble-wrap was invented. However, these life-saving medicines are also wrapped in mercy. Thousands of four-inch dolls are knitted by volunteers. They were the inspiration of a mother whose soldier son was killed by a landmine. Her son had previously found a young child, also dead through a landmine disaster, clutching a shattered plastic doll.

Social justice requires strategies of intense thought. Yet, if the accompaniment of mercy is absent it could be compared to a Saviour on a cross with only sacrifice on his mind. Our salvation was wrapped in a merciful sacrifice with arms wide open.

Motivation

When you face injustice are you thinking, 'Here I am', or 'There you are'?

Freeing the Oppressor

'I will give half my wealth to the poor, Lord, and if I have overcharged people on their taxes, I will give them back four times as much!' (v. 8).

Repentance motivated through being caught is often short-lived. In the realm of injustice what needs nailing to the wall is the abuse of power.

There was a man named Zacchaeus who is described as most influential in the Roman tax-collecting business. As a result he had become very rich. His career path sounds respectable but match it with his confession. The term 'most influential' requires interpretation. The use of power can be defined as abuse. Power is abused when it is used self-centredly by and for the individual, rather than for the community. Power is abused through domination, manipulation, disguise or privilege. Therefore, one of the purposes of The Salvation Army's International Social Justice Commission is to 'Lament the abusive and unethical behaviour imposed on vulnerable people in today's world'.

We hear Zacchaeus in his tones of lament. He thinks twice before declaring himself and picks a vantage point to muse over his position. He is not of basketball-player height so he climbs a tree to watch his source-of-income crowd surrounding the friend of sinners – Jesus.

If justice does not challenge human inequity it holds the pillars of faith and mercy as mere agents of charity. Transformational development hits root causes when hidden tree-climbers are faced and told to come down to discuss their perpetration of corruption.

The result of Jesus looking up into the face of duplicity was an enemy brought to his senses. Jesus wraps up the story well when he infers that Zacchaeus is lost and needing salvation. Victims of abusive power need justice to name the injustice.

Confrontation

To free the oppressed, one must face the oppressor.

Reputations at Risk

'The woman was surprised, for Jews refuse to have anything to do with Samaritans. She said to Jesus, "You are a Jew and I am a Samaritan woman. Why are you asking me for a drink?"' (v. 9).

Out-of-the-ordinary behaviour surprises us, especially from people labelled by their race, lifestyle or gender. Engaging with so-called dubious characters may raise questions. The encounter recorded in John 4 strikes an initial chord of suspicion. Jesus, as a man, dares to risk his reputation by engaging on his own with a woman of questionable virtue. He is tired and thirsty, and presumably hungry, as his disciples are away looking for food.

The nature of relationships covers a variety of considerations. You are reaching out in one moment and becoming aware of your vulnerability in the next. Is Jesus at risk? Is the woman at risk?

Human trafficking is a very live issue and more than a matter of statistics. It trashes human lives. One headline concerning it reads: 'Children sold like cabbages.' Cabbages, at least, are used just once – victims of human trafficking are a commodity that can be used again and again.

Jesus treats the woman with respect. If we are concerned with victims of slavery, how do we respond? Do we click our tongues in disbelief, comment on the abhorrent behaviour but do no more than write a cheque to a charity?

Human trafficking would end tomorrow if the demand dried up. The courage of Jesus to engage at the risk of disrepute is what is required to break the back of exploitation. The conversation which began with the subject of water ended with talk of spirit and truth. We must be willing to engage similarly.

Courage

Stake your reputation on being misunderstood for all the right reasons.

Our Jerusalem Trail

'But as he came closer to Jerusalem and saw the city ahead, he began to weep' (v. 41).

Responding to the call to be a public Church requires transparency without compromise. As we view Jesus on his journey we regret along with him that so many observers missed the essence of his identity. His inner thoughts reverberated with each step: 'How I wish today that you of all people would understand the way to peace. But now it is too late, and peace is hidden from your eyes' (v. 42).

The way of peace seems elusive and Jesus is emotionally upset. He knows cross-shaped rejection is ahead. The Jerusalems of this world are those daunting experiences of life that are inescapable. Tears flow in the acceptance of inevitable grief. Yet the picture is incomplete unless we pick up on Luke's observation of Jesus: 'As the time drew near for him to ascend to heaven, Jesus resolutely set out for Jerusalem' (9:51).

Nevertheless, the terrors of injustice create an emotion that strengthens resolve – something like Father Henri Nouwen's phrase 'wounded healers'. My own life has fluctuating points of deep emotion and strong determination, juxtaposing a rhythm of facing injustice with new possibilities.

In his life, Nelson Mandela carried the cross of apartheid to a prison cell. His long confinement took him onto the world's stage. Those who step out into the unknown with tears and determination line the Via Dolorosa in a way they could never imagine until it happens.

Ascension

Worshipping the resurrected Jesus returns us to the Jerusalem trail with great joy.

Jesus Shall Reign

'My anointed one will be a light for my people. He will be a glorious king' (vv. 17, 18, NLT).

Psalm 132 is not attributed. The author might have been Solomon, David, another king, or exiles who, having returned from captivity, mused on what God did in the past even as they longed for the restoration of the temple and everything it symbolised. Even if written long before their time, it could have been a favourite song of the returnees.

We sense that the psalmist fears the Davidic covenant and line could be broken and that would be devastating for God's people (vv. 11, 12). When childless King Hezekiah lay on what looked to be his deathbed God assured him that his covenant would be kept. This may be one of the psalms Hezekiah wrote.

We read of patriarch David's concern for God's house at two stages: first, when he arranged for the ark of the covenant to move from its temporary quarters in the field to a singular pavilion he'd prepared for it in Jerusalem (2 Samuel 6); second, when David purposed to build a permanent temple for the ark (2 Samuel 7).

Besides the importance of God's chosen leader, the psalm expresses the import of God's sanctuary. Verses 8–10 use some of the expressions Solomon used in his prayer when he dedicated the temple that his father had envisioned (2 Chronicles 6:41, 42). The psalmist glorifies the sovereign and the sanctuary.

Some of the answers to renewed petitions are in the text. Each time, God gives more than is requested. Verse 9 harks back to the Israelites' appeal when David brought the ark in from the field – that God's priests be clothed with righteousness and his saints shout for joy. Now in verse 16 God promises they'll be clothed with *salvation* and the saints shout *aloud* for joy. 'Righteousness in the pulpit and rejoicing in the pew combine to make a victorious church anytime.'[6]

Since the final verses point to the eventual reign of the ultimate ruler, the psalm is Messianic. The mighty God of Jacob and the descendant of David are one in the victorious Christ who shall reign for ever. Hallelujah!

Longing Engenders Vision

'Then I saw a new heaven and a new earth, for the old heaven and earth had disappeared. And the sea was also gone' (v. 1).

The apostle John creates a vision of pristine sparkle. In moves the new and out moves the old. Evil is painted out of the picture in the disappearance of the sea. In the book of Revelation, the sea and Satan become synonymous.

In the late 1800s The Salvation Army's founder, William Booth, went beyond words to depict his passion for justice. I have a copy of his dream painting where an angry sea is overwhelming the victimised masses of humanity. Looking at this vivid depiction you are impulsively drawn into the sea, wanting to jump in to 'rescue the perishing'. But as your imagination hits the icy waters your brave intentions begin to fade as you find yourself out of your depth.

Drowning in injustice has an unintended outcome. So how do we recast the new heaven and new earth that John envisages? Antoine de Saint-Exupéry said that if you want to build a ship you should not drum up the men to gather the wood, divide the work and give orders. Instead, you should teach them to yearn for the vast and endless sea.

Effective vision is multi-focused. It looks at the sea and builds, then looks at the sea and keeps building. Often we focus in isolation on our systems in defeating injustice. We yearn for bigger rescue boats which never slip out of dry dock for want of an informed vision of the sea. Defeat is inevitable unless those with the tools engage with a hope that goes beyond the preparation.

Just imagine

'No eye has seen, no ear has heard; and no mind has imagined what God has prepared for those who love him.'

(1 Corinthians 2:9)

All Postal Codes

'I heard a loud shout from the throne saying, "Look, God's home is now among his people! He will live with them, and they will be his people. God himself will be with them" ' (v. 3).

When God is linked to a place, it is often heaven, the kingdom of God, the holy city and so forth. The idea of 'the home of God' as given here is intriguing. We are given the picture of God making himself at home with his people – perhaps sitting back and joining in our conversation.

Social justice, at best, forms community from the inside out. Until you have been in someone's home you are a mere acquaintance. Walking through the front door of the place where others relax, co-exist and sleep for the night is revealing. Guards are let down, unless we are attempting to impress.

I have sat in the most humble of dwellings with the warmest of friends. On offer is more than mere hospitality. It's not just a social occasion. We are considering causes that disturb us. We unpack our uncertainties by building on our mutual trust.

When injustice strikes our world, it does so at the core of our being, turning our home into a place that is no longer safe. When hunger, abuse, nakedness, cold, unbearable heat, fear or sickness enters a home, it strikes at the core of our security. Thank God every home is in God's address book.

Homecoming

God's permanent address is not church – it is our home.

Live, Work, Reach, Believe

'He will wipe away every tear from their eyes and there will be no more death or sorrow or crying or pain' (v. 4).

If social justice from God's perspective provides a new heaven and a new earth, then the closing of the gap has a way to go. When does eternal life begin? How much sorrow, death, tears and pain is unnecessary! Let there be life on earth and let it begin with me.

The prayers of Francis of Assisi are a good place to start. Francis asked God to make him an instrument of God's peace. Francis also prayed:

May God bless you with discomfort at easy answers, half truths, and superficial relationships;
So that you may live deep within your heart.
May God bless you with anger at injustice, oppression and exploitation of people;
So that you may work for justice, freedom and peace.
May God bless you with tears to shed for those who suffer pain, rejection, hunger and war;
So that you may reach out your hand to comfort them and to turn their pain into joy.
And may God bless you with enough foolishness to believe that you can make a difference in the world;
So that you can do what others claim cannot be done to bring justice and kindness to all our children and the poor. Amen.

In touch

Discomfort, anger, tears and foolishness are the beginnings of social redemption.

God's Uncaged Bird

'And there will be no night there – no need for lamps or sun – for the Lord God will shine on them. And they will reign for ever and ever' (v. 5).

At certain times of the year the northern reaches of my homeland, Canada, live out Revelation 22:5. There is perpetual light twenty-four hours a day. The children don't want to go to bed, as looking outdoors they see a wideawake world even at midnight. We adults, however, get tired and welcome the darkness of night, when lights-out lulls us into escape from a worried weariness.

It's difficult to imagine a world without darkness. Picture with me the opening of The Salvation Army's International Social Justice Commission through a central theme of a bird in a cage. The beginning of the ceremony had children on the stage drawing colourful birds on canvasses. In thick black strokes the teacher artist drew a caged bird with a sad look on its face. An artistic dance showed the bird with bound wings, until the bindings were untied. The dance was not an instant contrast of flightless captivity to soaring heights. Learning to fly again was a transitional release of incremental take-offs.

The audience then silently filed into the Peace Garden of the Justice Centre. A live bird captured in a cage was to dramatise the effect of release. I unlatched the cage. I whispered to the bird: 'Do you want to come out?' My voice was invitational, gentle and anticipatory. Out came the bird, feet planted outside the cage, and then, whoosh – it soared up and up. It was drawn to the sunlit sky with the healing of height in its wings.

For a moment, just a moment, I saw people as birds outside the cages of their world but still unable to fly. The light is one matter but the face of God with its glow of encouragement is the lifter of broken wings.

Transformational Change

'I have not kept the good news of your justice hidden in my heart; I have talked about your faithfulness and saving power. I have told everyone in the great assembly of your unfailing love and faithfulness' (v. 10).

The Psalms are often earmarked to be sung by the temple choir. The words express emotions of joy, sadness, doubt or anger at injustice. So we begin to conclude our series with a crying out to the Lord for the abandoned of the world. We wait patiently for the Lord to bend down and hear our cry.

World views on some aspects of justice remain entrenched. Clever analysis of situations is not enough and we must be faithful to God in our speaking out against the unacceptable status quo. The prayer of our hearts merges with the expectancy of our faith that God's light will shine on the darkness of the world.

Our confidence to speak out comes from our knowledge of the power of God's Holy Spirit. The biblical story reflects the reality of the world's predicament. Scripture speaks through us with conviction and a relevance which leads us to agree with words of UN diplomat and reformer Eleanor Roosevelt:

> You gain strength, courage and confidence by every experience in which you really stop to look fear in the face. You are able to say to yourself, I lived through the horror. I can take the next thing that comes along. You must do the thing you think you cannot do.

Breaking the denial

To say we have always done it that way is to ground our words in fear of transformational change.

New Songs

'He has given me a new song to sing a hymn of praise to our God' (v. 3).

When I met a young choir at the United Nations building in Vienna, the choir members, seeing my Salvation Army uniform for the first time, gathered round me and asked many questions. Their country was not one that allowed free expression of the Christian faith. Despite the lack of a common language, we managed to communicate somehow.

Between meetings I stood on the piazza listening to them as they sang, so beautifully, their national folk songs. Not understanding their language, the words made no sense to me, but I suddenly realised that the tune of one of their songs was the same tune Christians in a number of denominations use for the hymn, 'We are marching in the light of God'!

Listening to and watching those children singing reminded me of the occasion when my sister and I had to sing a duet in church when we were young enough to be utterly nervous and self-conscious. We sang 'O come to my heart, Lord Jesus, There is room in my heart for thee', and whenever my sister and I hear that song today, so many years later, we smile and recall the occasion.

The world needs to hear songs. It particularly needs to hear the songs referred to by theologian Walter Brueggemann, who said: 'Only where there is doxology [hymns of praise to God] can there be justice, for such songs transfigure fear into energy.'

The spoils of injustice are uncaged when hearts sing to the God of justice: 'O come . . .'

A Suitable Diet

'But solid food is for the mature, who by constant use have trained themselves to distinguish good from evil' (Hebrews 5:14).

Between David's claim that his heart isn't haughty and his advice to God's people to hope in the Lord, he says: 'I have calmed and quieted myself, like a weaned child who no longer cries for its mother's milk' (v. 2, *NLT*). How is his soul like a weaned child's?

In times and places where mother's milk was the best available nourishment for a child, nursing would continue much longer than it usually does today. When he was weaned (aged three or older), Hannah took Samuel, her answer to prayer for a child, to the Lord's house to learn to assist Eli.

Well after she could eat table food, a young child still wanted her mother's milk, although she didn't need it. Whether seeking her mother's attention now shared with her baby brother, or looking for comfort, the two-year-old could be very insistent. She was not mature enough to be content without it.

A child who is weaned has completed a stage of development and is fulfilled, not clamouring. Life is full of new discoveries. She realises that varieties of food and drink can delight and satisfy.

As new believers, at first we need and crave milk (1 Peter 2:2). But solid food is for those maturing in the faith (Hebrews 5:14). Life presents opportunities for spiritual development, for discovering the enrichment of the word and a life of growth through obedience. As we learn to know who we are in the Lord, like David, we can choose to leave behind things such as prideful aims. We can choose to fret less and trust the Lord more. David speaks from experience. He knows that he can count on the Lord as his helper, as do we.

Eric Liddell, about whom *Chariots of Fire* was written, was said to have taught fellow prisoners in China in the Second World War his favourite hymn. Its words could echo today's psalm:

> Be still, my soul: the Lord is on thy side.
> Bear patiently the cross of grief or pain.
> Leave to thy God to order and provide;
> In every change, he faithful will remain.
>
> *Katharina von Schlegel*

Prayer Warriors

Introduction

Around the world, this year's newly commissioned Salvation Army officers (ministers) carry the session name of Prayer Warriors. Although they may be on different continents or speak different languages they share the one common name, and existing Salvation Army officers welcome reinforcements bearing such a helpful name who live it out.

General Shaw Clifton, The Salvation Army's world leader, says of the Prayer Warriors: 'Here is a name in keeping with the great need of our time. Prayer is the Army's spiritual engine and the need for those who will be constant and persistent in prayer is as urgent as ever it was. Prayer is a vital weapon in the Salvation War, a war we pursue without guns, and led by the Prince of Peace.'

Told of his grandfather's death, a young boy was heard to ask, 'Who will pray for me now?' He was very aware of the faithfulness and efficacy of the saintly man's prayers for him. Happily he has been supported by others in his considerable Christian family.

When we know we're prayed for it encourages and enables us. As I write *Words of Life* I'm grateful that, in the words of John Elliot's song, 'Lord, I believe somebody's prayin' for me'. Prayer is God's idea and he means Christians to use it for the sake of others as well as to develop our relationship with him.

The Quaker Rufus Jones said prayer is like the water in a lock through which a ship travels. The water rises and lifts the vessel so it can continue along a river at a new level. It's another way of saying what Jesus said about intentionally and privately spending time with God.

Even into her retirement, Salvation Army officer Lieut-Colonel Mina Russell taught widely on the subject of prayer. Reviewing notes from her classes in preparation for this series has been a prayer primer for me, and a mini refresher course.

The model prayer warrior, Jesus, lives to intercede for us (Hebrews 7:25). Someone depends on each of us as well. We share these thoughts to encourage our commitment and enliven our mission as prayer warriors.

Pray to Whom?

'Now all glory to God, who is able, through his mighty power at work within us, to accomplish infinitely more than we might ask or think' (v. 20).

'What we believe about God determines how we pray,' Lieut-Colonel Mina Russell stated at the outset of her seminars on prayer which I attended before becoming a Salvation Army officer. The notes I made then continue to prove timeless. What she taught grew out of her reading, Bible study, counselling and personal experience. If we accept her premise, it is essential to consider what we believe about God.

We believe that God is. The writer of the Letter to the Hebrews says, 'Anyone who comes to him must believe that he [God] exists and that he rewards those who earnestly seek him' (11:6).

God is eternal, yet contemporary; his name is I AM. He is not bound by time as we are, yet he is in the present moment. His eternity can help us to see an eternal viewpoint. Just as he is not limited by time, he is not limited by space. He is everywhere present. Mina Russell said, 'We pray in the presence, not in the absence of God.'

We believe that God is right. He doesn't need to change or to make course corrections. People need to change. If we are willing to follow his principles, we can live with fewer mistakes. If we intentionally seek his way, meaning to obey, he will give us trustworthy, fulfilling direction.

We believe that God is all-powerful and not just a human being in magnified form. He is able to deliver us, to keep us steady, to help us keep his promises, to give us grace, to do more than we can imagine.

We believe that God is love, and that fact assures us that we can pray without fear or in a demanding way. God works in answer to our prayers if they comply with the design he's given for effective praying.

If we believe these things about God, and want what he wants for us, we'll learn to co-operate with him and learn the broader scope of prayer.

Prayer His Way

'Open up before GOD, keep nothing back; he'll do whatever needs to be done' (v. 5, MSG).

God doesn't leave us to our own devices regarding prayer. He gives direction in the Bible. It is helpful to consider how our own prayers line up with Scripture.

In John 14–16 Jesus teaches us to pray in his name. He isn't laying down a compulsory style or providing a password. Rather he's asking that we consider whether our prayers are the kind he would pray. Do they have his tone, line up with his character and have the qualities we would expect in his prayers? 'From now on, whatever you request along the lines of who I am and what I am doing, I'll do it. That's how the Father will be seen for who he is in the Son. I mean it' (John 14:13, *MSG*).

One of those qualities that we know we should emulate is praying for things consistent with God's will. Some of these are easy to determine. The Bible teaches that God wants everyone to be saved, so praying for a person's salvation is definitely God's will. Similarly we know that God wants his people to live holy lives. We can confidently pray to be more like him. But for some things, discovering God's will takes our willingness to carry out what he shows us step-by-step.

Prayer is God-directed. While not neglecting issues which the Holy Spirit impresses on us, effective prayer is often faith-sized and specific. Not that answers are as automatic as an escalator that deposits us on the next floor with minimum effort on our part. More often it is like climbing a flight of steps. We and the people for whom we pray regulate the pace. Prayer takes work – not only in the praying but also in realising the answers. It may cost us time, interest, money, involvement or something else, but it will cost us something.

It may sound contradictory, but the cost of prayer includes our release or commitment of the focus of our prayer request to the Lord, to allow him to work in his way and without our interference. Waiting for the Holy Spirit's gentle nudge is the key.

Praying Jesus' way includes praying lovingly for others and with a spirit of thanks to God which shows our reliance on his way.

Jesus' Prayer

'For yours is the kingdom and the power and the glory forever. Amen' (v. 13, NKJV).

Jesus' prayer life gave him consistent daily contact with his Father. For him it was as essential as breathing. His teaching about prayer made what was natural for him, yet mysterious to the disciples, accessible.

He taught that personal prayer should be private – in a place where the pray-er and God can be alone. This may be a simple matter for many, yet for others may require creative, purposeful planning.

Jesus taught that prayer should not be mindless repetition of phrases, insincere mouthing of words or focus on one's own worth. Although many believers know some prayers by heart, they are best used thoughtfully, not routinely. The words of the Jesus Prayer ('Lord Jesus Christ, Son of God, have mercy on me, a sinner') and the Lord's Prayer provide lovely patterns and can be unifying.

The Lord's Prayer covers so much in very few words. Despite its simplicity, or perhaps because of it, Jesus' model prayer carries ample meaning. It starts with acknowledging our dependence on our Father as the source of life and reminds us that his holiness deserves reverence. It recognises him as King of a long-awaited kingdom and asks for his reign in us.

He goes on with a pattern for petition. We and others need daily food. We also need God's forgiveness and a willingness to forgive others. Since we want to live in victory over sin, we ask that we be led away from temptation. Deliverance from evil may take many forms and may involve personal action against evils that threaten others. The prayer's doxology is a pattern for praising and honouring God.

Perhaps today is a good time to return to some well-worn prayers we've known for years and to pray them slowly and with a sense of the weight of their words.

To meditate:

If a musical arrangement of the Lord's Prayer is available, listen to it as part of a thoughtful personal prayer time this week.

Into the Pantry

'Shut the door behind you and pray to your Father in private' (v. 6, NLT).

We blog, text or tweet to stay in touch. Blogging allows extensive expression of opinion. Text-messaging and tweeting provide short, quick contacts with friends. Each can be likened to some form of praying. However, the type of prayer that listens for God's direction is different. We may choose the time and place, but we relinquish control of the agenda and speed of interchange.

Jesus prayed in various ordinary settings, in homes, in the upper room, on a mountain, in a river and on the cross. When he told his followers to find a place to pray, he wasn't describing a special building. He used the word 'closet' – although probably just a curtained pantry of the house. It was not a place with a holy ambience, but an accessible, everyday place to be alone with God.

When our children were young, they knew that if I had what they called my Bible bag, I needed some quiet time. That canvas bag held a clipboard with loose-leaf pages, my Bible and some type of prayer list. I could be in the living room or on the back step, in the car or on my bed. Wherever the bag and I were was my 'closet'.

The author of *The Autobiography of Prayer*, Albert Edward Day, suggested: 'Take off your hat, shut the door, open the window, fold your hands.'[7] Begin by focusing on God in private with as few distractions as possible. Then talk to him about everything. Listen for what he says. End with praise for his goodness and greatness.

George Mueller, who recorded more than 20,000 answers to prayer, found that he could 'shut the door' by opening the Bible and anticipating that God would say something to him.

People suggest many methods and aids to personal prayer time. The time of day and our choices and patterns for prayer may change throughout our spiritual journey, but our aim will be to spend time personally communicating with our Lord and receive what we need.

Do we stand, sit, kneel or lie prostrate for prayer? The stance of the heart is more important than the position of the body. And what about intruders – those things that flood our minds in the prayerful stillness? E. Stanley Jones and Samuel Brengle let them become God-prompts as subjects for prayer.

Lifelong Pattern

'Father, the time has come. Glorify your Son, that your Son may glorify you' (v. 1).

There are so many kinds of prayer. What are some of the types the Gospels tell us Jesus employed? His life reveals his pattern of prayer. He prayed when people would not believe in him, when John the Baptist was killed, before selecting his disciples, when he needed spiritual refreshment or confirmation of his Sonship, to honour God's provision, in blessing for his followers.

In the upper room Jesus prayed a prayer of completion (v. 4). How did he reach this point? He lived in intentional continued obedience to God in spite of alluring alternatives. He can help us to live that way, too, if we ask him. Also in the upper room Jesus prayed a prayer of consecration for the sake of his disciples, all of us (v. 19).

In the garden Jesus' prayer was one of hesitation as he faced the cost of bearing the sins of the world (Matthew 26:39). We can stand beside him when we face uncertain days and have critical questions. We can know his help in seeing things God's way. The rest of Jesus' prayer in the garden was one of acceptance, co-operation with God's will. There is no substitute.

All these prayers prepared Jesus for Calvary. On the cross he compassionately prayed for forgiveness for his enemies (Luke 23:34). He shows us the way to cope with being wronged. We don't forget, but with forgiveness comes relief from the painful throb. Instead of an open wound, we can have a clean scar.

Jesus also prayed his wrenching question of loss and loneliness from the cross: 'About the ninth hour Jesus cried out in a loud voice . . . "My God, my God, why have you forsaken me?"' (Matthew 27:46). These are the opening words of Psalm 22. He used Scripture to voice his prayer.

We, too, find that in bleak situations when we don't know how else to frame our anguish, the words of others, especially those of the psalms, give us a voice. Jesus' prayer of commitment: 'Father, into your hands I commit my spirit' (Luke 23:46) illustrates that his desperate question did not shake his ultimate trust in God or God's love. In spite of our questions, God remains. Jesus prayed as the Son of Man and as the Son of God.

For Their Sakes

'For them I sanctify myself, that they too may be truly sanctified' (v. 19).

If I could know
That self-abandonment in me
Would help a man who never yet had prayed,
To speak to God –
If I could know
That giving self and time
Would bring the Christ to one who long had strayed
And lost his way –
If I could know ahead of time,
I'd give myself!

Not time alone – he has my days;
Not skills – he taught me all I know that he can use;
Not strength – from him it comes each hour.
But, if I knew ahead of time
That it would count in bringing men to God,
I'd give myself, my will, my heart,
I'm sure I would.

But as I live from day to day
I do not know how much my offering counts
In helping those I see.
Sometimes I catch a glimpse of God
At work through me;
But I have learned a little of the way of love,
The path of faith,
The road Christ followed to the cross,
And I must follow him
For his, and for their sakes.

And as he died for those who would forsake,
And those who would deny,
As well as for the strong who followed to the death,
I, too, must set myself apart,
For them, and for his sake,
Not knowing always what it means;
But sure that in this fellowship of love
I work with God –
And I can leave the end with him.

Mina Russell

What Are You Waiting For?

'I wait for the LORD, my soul waits, and in his word I put my hope' (v. 5).

Everyone knows what it feels like to wait. We wait at the traffic lights, bus stops, in the ticket or take-away queue, at the doctor's surgery, on the telephone, online. We wait anxiously for medical test results and eagerly for a long-planned holiday; impatiently for the end of a demanding assignment and in anticipation for plant buds to open.

The psalmist says that as he waits for God, he puts his hope in God's word. He still waits, but with certainty – like a night watchman on duty, who knows his shift will be over when the morning comes. No wonder he counsels: 'O Israel, put your hope in the *LORD*, for with the *LORD* is unfailing love and with him is full redemption' (v. 7).

Writing in the American *War Cry*, Salvation Army poet Marlene Chase considers our key verse and what waiting for answers to prayer can mean:

A Prayer at Times

I have respect for your timing, Lord –
in retrospect.
But at the moment of my yearning,
when need is burning in my bones,
my spirit groans
with urgent pleas and rigid rationale.
Passion all but consumes me
in a blazing ball of want.
Help me, Lord, to remember this,
not only in the bliss
of memory but now that your grace,
perfect like your timing,
can teach my soul its pace.

Others Queue

'Jesus healed many who had various diseases. He also drove out many demons' (v. 34).

Although we agree with Episcopal priest Dr Sam Shoemaker's assertion: 'People should walk through our prayers in droves', and we could certainly include more people in our prayers than we do, most of the time the 'droves' need to move through one by one. I can pray in general for the victims of a disaster and the legion of volunteers who help them. But any results may be too general to grasp. Faith-sized, focused prayers allow us the joy of seeing answers by degrees and of being involved in some way with the people for whom we pray.

Anyone with whom we come in contact can be in the prayer queue. Family, friends, colleagues, healthcare professionals, public servants, leaders, people to or for whom we're responsible, neighbours, passing acquaintances. Many may not be Christians, so among other things we can pray for their hearts to be awakened to the love of God. As we pray for them we stay alert to God's guidance to us, and with the confidence that he will touch them in his way and time, not ours.

There may be more and more who are sick among those in our prayer queues. No one is impervious to illness. We want to 'fix' their situation, yet demanding God's healing may exhibit fear rather than faith. Placing the sick in God's hands and helping them to pray a similar prayer of release is more helpful. Although not sought, sometimes sickness is used for a special ministry. So much has been discovered about healing of mind and body that our prayer and the skills of physicians can work in health-giving co-operation.

We pray for fellow believers and sometimes are impressed to do so at unusual times. We wake in the night and can't get someone out of our minds. Often they live a great distance from us. We pray for them. Occasionally we may learn how important the timing was, but usually we don't. Yet God has allowed us to work with him for their good.

Prayer is a form of loving service to others. God's love works in us and his gift of faith through us to link those for whom we pray with God for their good and his glory.

Prayer, Limited

'For everyone who exalts himself will be humbled, and he who humbles himself will be exalted' (v. 14).

One helpful preparation for living cross-culturally is studying sociograms of host cultures and adapting our expectations accordingly. Individuality and independence are highly valued in some societies while the harmony of the group is most important in others. Our self-sufficiency can limit effectiveness in prayer too.

Although the Bible teaches that God wants our co-operation, he does not want us to take over. We assume we can forge ahead based on our experience, and proceed without his guidance. But even similar people and situations are never exactly alike. We need God's direction. His comprehension of the need and its eternal significance is full, ours partial.

Self-defence can limit our prayers. We may excuse a stubborn will or character flaw and be unwilling to get close to God and his holiness, lest something more be expected from us. Self-defence can take the form of self-righteousness. It may even keep us from missing a sense of God's presence.

In Luke 18, Jesus' illustration of prayer centres around the attitudes of two people who visited the temple. One stood by himself, possibly to draw attention to his prayer and its theme, his worthiness. The *NKJV* says that he 'prayed with himself' (v. 11). The other person stood at a distance with bowed head and heart and in humble and sorrowful words acknowledged his unworthiness and prayed for mercy. Jesus said it was this man who went home right with God.

Power in prayer is a by-product, not prayer's main aim. An attitude of love for God is expressed through staying in accord with him and wanting his way. Being lost in God is the surest way of finding his limitless strength for our day.

Thee we would be always blessing,
Serve thee as thy hosts above;
Pray and praise thee without ceasing,
Glory in thy perfect love.
Charles Wesley (*SASB* 438)

Prayer, Unlimited

'I am the vine; you are the branches. If a man remains in me and I in him, he will bear much fruit; apart from me you can do nothing' (v. 5).

Paul urges us to pray continually (1 Thessalonians 5:1). We don't do so in order to avoid duties or to shift them onto others. Rather prayer precedes and follows assignments as well as springing up in the midst of them. When prayer becomes our default setting, we are more frequently spiritually attentive in everything.

Praying continually includes using little breaks of time to pray instead of worrying about the delayed response, the wait at the grocery store or in traffic, the periods of wakefulness at night.

The Global Positioning System (GPS) beams its mapping information from a satellite to Earth so that potentially anyone in the world may benefit. Yet collecting the data requires a GPS receiver. Beyond that, someone must switch on the receiver to tap into its information and then request the best route for keeping on track on a journey. The needed directions become useful when they are followed, especially through unfamiliar areas. Prayer is part of a Christian's GPS of sorts, giving us connection to God to determine what is needed next.

It is not incessantly talking to God or endlessly repeating our petitions or a formulated prayer. Rather, it is awareness of God's omnipresence and of his willingness to speak to us. It is the posture of hearts listening for direction from the One who loves us most and staying in contact with his power beyond ourselves.

Prayer is our heart's desire. It is acknowledgement of our dependence on God, our source. It is willing submission to the One we trust to work in our best interests. It is a fellowship of the human spirit with the Spirit of God (Romans 8:26, 27). It is an intentional, confident turning of ourselves toward him. It is our means of confession of selfishness and sin. It gives us a glimpse of God's splendour and provides a way to co-operate with God's will.

Prayer gives power, strength and peace. It accomplishes impossible things, overcomes fear, gives us perspective and affects the hearts of others.

Jesus' illustration of the relationship of branches to the vine in John 15 is a picture of the fruitful fellowship of praying continually.

Everyone Participates, Everyone Profits

'They devoted themselves to the apostles' teaching and to the fellowship, to the breaking of bread and to prayer' (Acts 2:42).

If our solitary prayers have ripple effects beyond our expectations, how much more do the prayers of believers joined in prayer fellowship. The early Church began in a prayer meeting of people who obeyed Jesus' instruction to wait in Jerusalem for the promised Holy Spirit. The inner circle of disciples and women and many others who followed Christ steadfastly persisted in prayer together.

For 120 people to be in one accord was an answer to prayer in itself. Reaching that type of oneness prepared them for the start of a powerful outreach which continues today. Initially 3,000 of the crowd who heard the outdoor sermon believed on the day of Pentecost. Yet they couldn't meet by the thousands, but in necessarily smaller numbers as gathering in private homes dictated.

The Church in China continues to grow in part because of restriction on the size of house churches. When there are more than twenty-five members, the government insists that the house church splits. Unwittingly, the government helps to replicate the growth pattern of the first-century Church.

In recent years the Church in the West has emphasised small-group, single-focus ministries. These include prayer groups which employ creative approaches such as prayer rooms with places for expression in many forms. One Salvation Army corps (church) in England started a weekly knitting prayer ministry in which people who knit together pray for the recipients of their shawls, hats and toys – some known, but many unknown to the knitters.

A prayer group decided to pray conversationally and set down a plan. They all prayed about one subject at a time whether aloud or silently. The prayers were very short and used everyday language. As much as possible, they were specific about people and situations. They allowed for silence, which meant they could keep confidences and wait for guidance.

Rosalind Rinker, author of *Prayer: Conversing with God*, suggested four simple things to remember in small-group prayer: God is here; thank you, Lord; help me, Lord; help my brother. No group is too small to meet meaningfully with the Lord (Matthew 18:20).

Companion of Christ

'I pray also for those who will believe in me through their message' (v. 20).

Jesus prayed in many places and circumstances. John records one of Christ's prayers for his followers. The twelve were sometimes obtuse, without faith and selfish. Jesus loved them and prayed for them even though he knew they would forsake him for a time. We don't naturally take the same attitude as Christ until we learn more of his sacrificial love.

He wanted the best for them. He didn't condemn them, but brought them to God with awareness of what they could become. In his concern he prayed that they would have joy (v. 13), be protected (v. 15) and be sanctified (v. 17). Christ expanded his prayer to include any who would come to believe in him through them. He prayed that we too would be one (v. 21), be mature (v. 23), see his glory (v. 24) and would learn to love (v. 26).

Do we feel urged to pray for someone? That is the needed seed. It grows as we pray for them and visualise their potential in God. Some people won't allow others to get close, but God can use our prayer to reach them and open them to him. Can we dare to believe for people who seem hopeless, irritable or difficult to understand?

Pause to pray for someone close at hand – a co-worker, an awkward saint, a family member or acquaintance who is difficult to understand. Pray that God's love will reach them in a way they can comprehend, that God will touch them in his way.

Pause to pray for someone far away – a relative, friend or missionary – that our faith and love will reach them today.

Through prayer God benefits us as well as those for whom we pray. God communicates his love for us so that we can learn to love like Jesus loves. God gives us strength to overcome our weaknesses and to encourage others. God shows us his way and his wisdom to help us to live blamelessly. God gives us perspective. God gives us his Spirit to help us represent him effectively.

To pray:

Thank you, Lord, for your design for companionship with you – prayer.

Hindrances and Helps

'Praise be to God, who has not rejected my prayer' (v. 20).

The Bible refers to hindrances to prayer. Unconfessed sin is a hindrance (v. 18). Jesus made moral demands of those seeking spiritual answers. Although sometimes the prayers of the unsaved may be answered, the only prayer of the unsaved which is certain to be answered is one for salvation.

Selfishness can be a reason for unanswered prayer (James 4:3). It appears in a number of forms besides asking for things for ourselves. It may show up in a high opinion of our rights. It may reveal itself in a desire to control others. It may appear in an attitude of jealousy or superiority.

Another hindrance to prayer is a lack of love. Jesus reminds us that loving God with all we have and our neighbour as ourself is uppermost (Matthew 22:37–40). Do our prayers match the standard of love in 1 Corinthians 13: sincere, kind, patient, humble, considerate, tender, generous, confident and constant? If our prayers lack Christlike love, perhaps we need to revisit Calvary where we were forgiven by limitless love.

Jesus spoke about our willingness to forgive as a condition of being forgiven. We are forgiven by one who knows us intimately, yet loves and forgives us. If we withhold forgiveness we stand in judgement, pride and intolerance of others. God can show us how to let his love heal and reconnect us.

Whether out of fear or misconceived assumptions, lack of readiness to obey God can be a hindrance to prayer. Willingness to go God's way, to forgo personal preferences, to ask 'Is this what Jesus would do?' are some signs that we're ready to obey God.

If we lack faith when we pray, it may be because we are looking within or around us rather than to our invincible Lord. Jesus' prescription for a clear view of God is purity of heart (Matthew 5:8). We can realise his presence even though we cannot see him.

J. I. Packer said:

> For God's children, 'Ask and you will receive' is always true, and what they receive when they ask is always God's best for them long-term, even when it is a short-term disappointment. Some things in life are certain, and that is one of them.[8]

Fortified

'Many a time and much have they afflicted me . . . yet they have not prevailed against me' (v. 2, AB).

We don't know who the author of the psalm is. Some date it after the captivity when a group who returned to rebuild Jerusalem were harassed and opposed by surrounding foes. Whether applied to Israel, to the Church or to lives of individual followers of Christ, Psalm 129 offers key reminders.

One section of the psalm recalls both Israel's affliction from the beginning and God's deliverance from those who opposed him, his people and his plans. The other section affirms that the plans of the enemies of God and his purposes may appear to flourish temporarily, but are flimsy and will never ultimately triumph.

From other Old Testament references, we infer that Israel's youth began during her slavery in Egypt. The psalmist's strong word picture of ploughing their backs (v. 3) may have meant cruel treatment in general or literal scourging by slave-masters. Another interpretation is that the Israelites were yoked and coerced to pull ploughs in place of the customary animals. This fits with the next verse in which an uncompromisingly righteous God has cut them loose from their binding cords.

At the start the psalmist calls Israel to remember and to declare that the enemy has not prevailed. He concludes that those who hate God and all he represents come to nothing. Earlier he used a strong word picture of people being harshly used for work like animals. By marked contrast, he compares the wicked to wispy grass.

He accentuates the frail state of something the wind may have planted on a grass roof. It withers before it is fully grown or before the traditional harvest salutation and blessing can be offered. Not only will the evil one not prevail, his endeavours will fail.

Can we apply this psalm's principles today? Recall the times you have lived through affliction and the Lord has delivered you or accompanied you, and let that encourage your faith for today's challenges. Do those who reject or ignore God seem to spring up all around us? It's heartening to remember that their schemes are transient and God will have the final word. God's unfaltering, victorious presence in our past and future fortifies us today.

Give Me or Make Me?

'And to know this love that surpasses knowledge – that you may be filled to the measure of all the fulness of God' (Ephesians 3:19).

The story Jesus told in Luke 15 focuses on a young person, full of ambition and centred on himself and his belongings. We notice this when he says, 'Give me my share' (v. 12) and then soon gathers his things and is off to enjoy himself without restraint (v. 13). When he is ruined, he rethinks his options and returns home, humbled. Now he intends to confess his unworthiness and to ask his father, 'Make me like one of your hired men' (v. 19). The difference in his verbs reflects his change of heart.

Our initial 'make me' prayer was probably for salvation. As growing believers, do our prayers tend more to the 'give me' type or have we realised our need, and now trust the Father's goodness as we ask him to 'make me' what he wants us to be?

I brought to God a question long withheld,
A question which had oft disturbed my peace.
The answer would have settled all my doubts,
Or so I often thought before release.

But when there came no answer and no voice,
I left it with the Christ, went out in fear;
And then, I found the peace of mind I sought
In faith, in trust – not in an answer clear.

And somehow with my trust an answer came,
Not to the haunting question now so dim,
But to the large eternal things of life,
As daily I kept pace and walked with him.

Mina Russell

To ponder:

'What did you bring me?' the child in us asks. 'Myself,' the Lord replies as he enfolds us and we are completely satisfied.

Pray it Forward

'Pray every way you know how, for everyone you know' (v. 1, MSG).

A woman retired as chaplain of a hospital in Georgia, USA. Among the things she did regularly for thirty years was to go from staff member to staff member praying a blessing on them and the work of their hands in the hospital. One day in a windowless room she encountered a worker whose job was to select and bundle the surgical instruments ordered for the procedures to be performed in the operating rooms that day. She told the chaplain that as she gathered the tools, she noted the patients' names and prayed for the patients in anticipation of their surgery.

How can we apply this principle in our tasks? How can we 'pray it forward'? As I write today's thoughts more than a year before you will read them, I am praying for you.

Those paying attention to the FIFA competition are following events in South Africa this month as World Cup results unfold. Perhaps some have prayed for those involved in Street Child World Cup which took place ahead of the FIFA event. It was organised by a network of groups led by a Christian-based human rights charity, Amos Trust. Rather than shipping the street children out of sight while the world's attention converged on the World Cup, this year some of those children participated in their sport and were allowed to raise issues affecting them in a forum in which they'd be heard.

Another worldwide gathering with tremendous potential is approaching. During 15–18 July, 1,000 Salvationists aged eighteen to twenty-eight will attend a world youth convention in Stockholm, Sweden. We pray for them as they travel and gather in this unique forum, that their understanding of mission will be challenged, their commitment to God and his call to holy living and Christlike service affirmed.

We pray also for the couple of dozen of the convention delegates who will spend the two weeks prior to going to Sweden in an intensive holiness and service seminar in London.

In praying for all the delegates, we extend our faith into the future for God's activity through The Salvation Army. Let's join in prayer for the 'Raised-Up' convention before, during and after it is in session. Imagine the possibilities of 'praying it forward'!

Inner Life of God's People

'And pray in the Spirit on all occasions with all kinds of prayers and requests. With this in mind, be alert and always keep on praying for all the saints' (Ephesians 6:18).

One of the twelve calls issued by The Salvation Army's Spiritual Life Commission is a call to the inner life. As members together of the body of Christ, 'a people within the people of God', Salvationists worldwide are called to 'a renewal of faithful, disciplined and persistent prayer; to study God's word consistently and to seek God's will earnestly; to deny self and to live a lifestyle of simplicity in a spirit of trust and thankfulness'.[9]

Near the end of his Letter to the Colossians, Paul advises believers to be devoted to prayer in a watchful and thankful manner and to pray for his clear and proper proclamation of the message of Christ with continued open doors for that message. In a similar vein, the commission's report states: 'The vitality of our spiritual life as a Movement will be seen and tested in our turning to the world in evangelism and service, but the springs of our spiritual life are to be found in our turning to God in worship, in the disciplines of life in the Spirit, and in the study of God's word.'

Practically and perceptively the commission advises: 'It is possible to develop a prayer life which is removed from the way we live. Strange though it may seem, it is possible to develop a personally enriching time with the Lord, yet fail to translate this into our daily living. The question, "To what extent is my lifestyle an honest reflection of the prayers I speak?" is well worth answering.'

The commission also asks us to consider how we can ensure that our prayer life receives daily priority, that faithful, disciplined prayer remains at the heart of body life and that we remain open to new ways of cultivating our inner life.

While we consider these challenges, we do well to remember Scripture's caution as the final word on prayer: 'Do not be anxious about anything, but in everything, by prayer and petition, with thanksgiving, present your requests to God. And the peace of God, which transcends all understanding, will guard your hearts and your minds in Christ Jesus' (Philippians 4:6, 7). Amen!

Fifth-Century BC Journalism

A study of 1 Chronicles

Introduction

As we visit an Old Testament book not commented on in recent years – 1 Chronicles – we might feel we're entering a museum or library exhibition where the lighting is low to preserve the old manuscripts. Yet 1 and 2 Chronicles are part of Scripture and deserve our attention.

Until the Greek version of the Old Testament was compiled in about 200 BC, 1 and 2 Chronicles were one book in Hebrew manuscripts. But Greek, with its vowels, required more space.

We aren't certain of their author, who is known simply as the chronicler or writer of the account. Tradition holds that it probably is Ezra. As various New Testament writers built on other sources, we notice that passages of the Chronicles parallel many in 1 and 2 Samuel and 1 and 2 Kings. Yet they are not repetitious quotations.

It may prove helpful to turn to some of those sources while reading Chronicles. When the writer refers to the annals of the kings, official genealogies, the records of prophets such as Samuel, Nathan, royal letters, lamentations and the plans of the temple, he reveals careful attention to historical documents. We imagine him comfortably surrounded by stacks of scrolls in a scriptorium of sorts.

The chronicler is not a historian updating or rewriting Israel's past, but one who studies that history and draws lessons from it for the people and situations of his day, a people returned from exile. He's a journalist of sorts with the bias of one raised in a religious tradition. The writer may have been of the Levitical line, probably attached to the temple. He would have insight into the purpose of worship and its function and importance for the nation.

We start with an overview of the opening chapters.

Legacy of Faith

'Your kingdom is an everlasting kingdom, and your dominion endures through all generations' (Psalm 145:13).

As we saw in our study of Zechariah (June 2009), hope for the community that survived the exile and returned to Jerusalem, the city of David, was in the restoration of the temple and religious institutions. First Chronicles chapter 3 records David's royal line, including the kings of Judah and the royal line after the exile.

In 1 and 2 Chronicles, the emphasis on David, the priesthood, the temple and better days ahead would greatly encourage the returned exiles who lived in the midst of the rubble of their devastated city and the faded glory of their ancestors' faith.

Their sovereign God plans for redemption and reconciliation. He includes David in the plan in an unimaginable way when the Messiah, the greater David, comes as King and Priest. Even in the midst of rebuilding, the people of destiny have a history and a hope because of God's presence. Through weak or wavering faith, God's preserving grace prevails for those in covenant with him.

Since the emphasis is on David's line and the Levitical line, the first nine chapters of 1 Chronicles give genealogies to show that God's hand has been on Israel and Judah from the beginning. We start with an overview of these opening chapters. Peruse them if time permits. Today's reading highlights some of the duties of musical Levites and the high priests.

Many of us are fascinated with our family history. We use books, websites, official records, visits to cemeteries and more to fill in missing pieces of our family trees. We might likewise consider the roots and history of our Christian faith. John Coutts helps us take the wider view of Christianity in his slim paperback, *Saints Alive – a Brief History of the Christian Church.*[10]

We can trace our own spiritual heritage in our natural family or the church family. Who exampled the Christian life for you or brought you to Christ? Let's thank God for their lives and influence. We ponder how that legacy of faith will continue to be a living one as we turn to books written along similar lines 2,400 years ago.

Generations of Preparation

'He remembers his covenant for ever, the word he commanded, for a thousand generations' (Psalm 105:8).

In the first nine chapters the author lists nations, tribes and individuals who root God's redemption plan.

Chapter 1 – the writer lists notables such as Adam, Noah, Shem, Abraham, Isaac and Jacob. Then the wide angle narrows. Chapter 2 – after naming Jacob's twelve sons, we see Judah and his descendants through whom David would come. David and his immediate family are mentioned briefly in verse 15. The writer gives a side bar on another of Judah's descendents whose offspring's names correspond with many places in the land of Judah, possibly because they founded those towns. Of particular interest are Ephrathah and Bethlehem, birthplace of David and Jesus (vv. 51, 54).

Chapter 3 – with David included in the genealogy, we zoom in on David's own line. The list of Solomon's descendants is in effect a list of Judah's kings from Solomon through Zedekiah and their exilic and post-exilic continuation. Chapter 4 gives more of the line of the pre-eminent tribe, Judah. Chapter 5 holds family trees of the tribes of Reuben, Gad and Manasseh, all given land on the east side of the Jordan River.

Chapter 6 delineates the tribe of Levi including Moses, Aaron, Miriam and, generations later, Samuel the prophet–priest, and the roles they played. The writer gives special attention to those three families of this tribe who descended from Samuel's grandson – Heman, Asaph and Ethan – those whom David appointed as his chief musicians for worship. He re-emphasises Aaron's role as high priest, then carefully lists the places where the Levites were assigned to live.

Chapter 7 gives the rest of the genealogies of the tribes. Chapter 8 details the tribe of Benjamin because of its notable member, Saul, the first king of Israel, and continues through Saul's son, Jonathan, and grandson, Mephibosheth. Chapter 9 describes the duties of some of the first returnees from exile, priests, Levites and temple servants.

And Yet

'I trust in God's unfailing love for ever and ever' (Psalm 52:8).

After the lengthy genealogies, the writer sets the stage for the beginnings of the Davidic reign by detailing the death of David's predecessor, the first king of Israel, the Benjamite, Saul.

The writer presumes readers are familiar with Saul's life and his struggles with the Philistines. As a general he was decisive, courageous, persistent and frequently victorious. Even aside from his bouts of mental torment, as a ruler Saul was weak, easily jealous, fearful, suspicious and rash.

Saul's type of death is shown as God's judgement on his life of disobedience. He disobeyed God's explicit directions, did not truly seek the Lord and he went against well-known Jewish teaching by consulting a medium. When Saul sought out the witch's counsel, it was at Endor, situated at the foot of Mount Gilboa. The next day he was mortally wounded on Gilboa and fell on a sword which the Hebrew indicates was his armour bearer's.

This may have settled a score. Jewish tradition holds that Saul's armour bearer that day was Doeg the Edomite, who earlier informed the king about priests who helped David. When Saul's rash reaction was to kill eighty-five priests, Doeg carried it out. If the armour bearer at Gilboa was Doeg, then both the king and his aide fell by the weapon they'd used to massacre the priests of God.

When David heard of the senseless loss of life on his account, he did not seek revenge but wrote what is now Psalm 52, which spoke against Doeg's treachery. David went on to declare that he stood firm and flourished in God. He praised God for his love and help and hoped in his name alone.

Saul's death may be seen by some as justice for his treachery and unfaithfulness, but David finds it regrettable. Instead of rejoicing, he writes a soulful lament for Saul and Jonathan, David's best friend, then orders the men of Judah to learn the song (2 Samuel 1:17–27).

Even non-musicians can hear the echo of their heart's sadness, longings, determination and joys in the metre and melody of song. Neither tragedy nor injustice is for ever. With David, we hope in the name of the Lord and trust in his unfailing love.

Of Our Hands

'When you eat the labour of your hands, you shall be happy, and it shall be well with you' (v. 2, NKJV).

The psalmist makes it plain that all who revere God and live accordingly are truly fortunate people. Part of their happiness comes from the blessing of eating the labour of their own hands. Literally this could be food from their arbours or gardens. But it could also stand for their livelihood of whatever type. Something productive to do and the health to do it gives life significance. Opportunity to make an honest living is a simple mercy. In his letters, Paul reminds the Thessalonians and the Ephesians of the importance of living peacefully and making a living from working with their hands as he did. He said that the additional benefit would be the ability to give to those in need (Ephesians 4:28).

Using our hands productively is satisfying and reflects our Creator's activity. We ourselves are called God's handiwork, recreated in Christ for a purpose (Ephesians 2:10, *AB*). What do you consider to be the work of your hands? It might be growing or preparing food. It could be earning a living or helping others. Perhaps it's a hobby or a ministry of encouragement through correspondence. The works of our hands can be countless.

I wrote '21 August 1986' in my Bible beside verse 2 of our psalm. It reminds me of the date I received an advance copy of a magazine with an article I had written. Although occasionally asked to write prescribed programme material, this was the first time something I had initiated appeared in print. It was a signal and encouraging blessing on the work of my hands.

The psalmist says that those walking with God will have children in every corner of the house. For many, then and now, having plenty of children is a blessing. When premature death is frequent, progeny to carry on the family is important. Married or not, all believers have an opportunity and duty to nurture spiritual offspring. The Lord will show us how if we ask him.

To pray:

'Let the beauty of the LORD our God be upon us, and establish the work of our hands for us.'

(Psalm 90:17, NKJV)

Success in Welding a Kingdom

'And David became more and more powerful, because the LORD Almighty was with him' (v. 9).

Because the history was well known, the writer only briefly relates David's reign and his campaign to gain control over all of Israel. All Israel comes to David at Hebron (v. 1). We recall that he has already reigned over Judah for seven years. Israel now wants him as a ruler too and recognises his divine appointment. When the elders of Israel come to anoint David as king over Israel (v. 3), he makes a compact with them. This is probably an oath to be loyal to the expectations of a king that God gave Moses in anticipation of having a king in the Promised Land.

In Deuteronomy 17:18–20, one of those expectations was that he would write a copy of the God-given law the Levites kept. Typing that volume of text would be daunting let alone copying it by hand. We tend to remember thoughts we have captured with a pen.

Anyone who would hand-copy the law of the Lord would certainly inscribe it in his mind. The king was to keep that copy with him and read it all his life. This was to help him learn to revere God, follow his decrees, and not to think himself better than his fellow citizens.

David and his united forces march to Jerusalem and capture the city. All Israel has a share in taking the city, a strategic and neutral location between Judah and Israel. David makes the fortress his home and handles the development of the acropolis while his right-hand man, Joab, restores the remainder of the city. It becomes known as the city of David. Later it would become the holy city, the place of the temple and the political and religious focus of the kingdom.

In 1 Chronicles 11:10–47 the narrator emphasises the support David receives from select mighty men in carrying out the word and will of God concerning Israel. In supporting him, they strengthen themselves. His triumph is theirs. The majority of the strong, alert personalities who rally about David recognise his effective leadership qualities. They come from David's own area. .

David fully recognises that his success and theirs is ultimately from God. How do we credit ours?

Soldiers of the King

'Day after day men came to help David, until he had a great army, like the army of God' (v. 22).

The verses of the first half of chapter 12 could have chronologically followed 11:9. The narrator continues listing the brave and good men who join David at various points in his career. As followers add themselves to David's operation, the momentum grows and David's accession becomes more promising. By the close of the chapter there is a great feast as the broad base of support celebrates new joy in Israel.

A number who were Benjamites – of Saul's tribe – joined David even before Saul's death (vv. 1–7). Some of the new supporters were ambidextrous. Although an unusual ability even today, then it was valuable in shooting arrows and slinging stones.

David may doubt the motives and intentions of certain groups which attach themselves to his cause. While giving them the benefit of the doubt, he warns them to remain loyal or pay a dire price. No doubt David is relieved to hear what a leader of one such new group declares. Scripture says that Amasai speaks under the inspiration of the Spirit and assures David of his men's allegiance: 'We are yours, O David! We are with you, O son of Jesse! Success, success to you, and success to those who help you, for your God will help you' (v. 18). David would be even more impressed when their actions fitted the words.

As soldiers in the army of King Jesus we sing:

Soldiers in the Army,
Soldiers of the King,
Faith and dauntless courage
To his cause we bring.
May we never waver,
Strengthened by his might,
In his steps we follow,
In his name we fight.
Doris N. Rendell (*SASB* 866)

When we make known our allegiance to Christ and stand ready to follow his lead, he waits to see that commitment in action.

Not So Fast

'How can I ever bring the ark of God to me?' (v. 12).

David has his priorities straight. Once he's established Jerusalem as the capital of the newly united Israel, he wants to make it the religious centre as well. He consults with his representatives about the ark of the covenant which has been relegated to storage and neglected under Saul's reign. Understandably, David wants to give the ark, called by God's name and symbol of God's presence, a prominent and permanent place.

David and all Israel, self-assured that this is God's will (v. 4), move forward with the plan. David gathers everyone from the kingdom's southern border to its northern boundary to join in this joyful, religious procession. They go to the place about eight miles from Jerusalem where the ark has been kept for nearly a century since the Philistines returned it.

The Philistines had put the ark on a cart and let two unaccompanied milk cows that had never been yoked wander off with it. The cows should have turned back to their calves or bolted, but they went straight down the road lowing and arrived in the Israelite camp (1 Samuel 6:7–13). God guided its return.

Now the Israelites put the ark on a new cart and begin the parade in high spirits. A full complement of vocal and instrumental music aids their merry celebration before God. They intend to accompany it to Jerusalem. Their intentions are commendable, but their methods aren't.

Rather than using a cart, Levites should have carried the ark. That was the God-directed method of transport from the earliest tabernacle days (Exodus 25:13–15). No wonder when the oxen stumble and the ark shifts, Uzza tries to steady it. Since touching it was prohibited, tragedy ensues. The ark had been in Uzza's house all his life. He should have been aware of that caution.

David's displeasure turns to reverent fear of the Lord as he recognises what his imprudent haste and assumptions have caused. He abandons his plan and allows the ark to be held at a house nearby for three months. That period was one of constant blessing for the host family. No doubt David learned that God's direction outweighs human plans.

Obey and Trust

'And David knew that the LORD had established him as king over Israel and that his kingdom had been highly exalted for the sake of his people Israel' (v. 2).

David settles in and gathers materials to build a royal residence. He has a large family at a time when having many offspring is deemed a sign of God's blessing. When the chronicler names thirteen sons of David's many children, we especially note one, Solomon.

Contrary to moving ahead based only on the counsel of leaders, as he had done in his initial retrieval of the ark, in the instances about fighting the Philistines, David asks God for direction. God gives him the go-ahead as well as assurance that he will deliver them to David. No wonder when David vanquishes the enemy, he accurately assesses: 'God has broken out against my enemies by my hand' (v. 11). David emphasises God's primacy when he orders that the discarded images of the enemy's gods be burned.

When the Philistines raid the valley, David again asks God what to do. Divine direction is different this time. He's to turn away from the enemy and circle around near certain mulberry or balsam trees before going against them. He should wait to go to battle until he hears the sound of marching in the tree tops. David follows what must seem a strange instruction and waits for something no human can manufacture, the stirring in the trees.

We recall God's promise of victory and Joshua's similar obedience at Jericho when he was told to march the army, led only by blasts of seven trumpets and the ark, around the city for a week (Joshua 6). The great shout on the final march brought the walls down and gave the city to the Israelites. Likewise, God promised Gideon and an elite band victory over the Midianites with only trumpets, jars and torches (Judges 7).

David, ever ready to face what opposes God's people and purposes, demonstrates a transparent, mature faith as he waits for God's direction. He doesn't apply his preconceived plan or even what worked before. He doesn't second-guess God. He looks up, not just to the rustling of the tree tops, but to God and his way. Words from Augustus Toplady's hymn describe our readiness and God's enabling another way: 'But I can only spread my sail; thou must breathe the auspicious gale.'

Second Verse Better than the First

'So all Israel brought up the ark of the covenant of the LORD with shouts, with the sounding of rams' horns and trumpets, and of cymbals, and the playing of lyres and harps' (v. 28).

Once again David prepares to move the ark to Jerusalem and house it in a prominent place. He may have a grand building in mind for it, but for the present he will keep it under a special tent – perhaps reminiscent of the tabernacle in the wilderness.

This time David means to observe proper protocol in moving the ark (v. 2). He acknowledges that when they attempted to move the ark before, they failed because they neglected to ask the Lord for direction. Additionally, they didn't use the Levites to transport the ark as prescribed in the law (v. 13). When those God calls to minister are either passed over or neglect to serve, their absence in ministry affects others.

This time nearly 900 from the descendants of Levi prepare to retrieve the ark and escort it to Jerusalem. Some will function as pole bearers or honour guards, while others will be singers or instrumentalists. They all appropriately consecrate themselves for the task. We wonder if they did so with apprehension, considering what happened the first time David wanted to move the ark. They must have been greatly relieved and encouraged as they advanced without incident. They soon stop to offer sacrifices in gratitude to God (v. 26).

David shows his high regard for music when he gives attention to it in accompanying the ark's transfer (v. 16). Perhaps this also heralds his establishment of musical guilds and services in connection with worship at Jerusalem.

For its day, the joyful procession was bigger than a winning sports team's homecoming victory parade, and more respectful. David included all the leaders of the people in the event. No doubt the memory of the sights and sounds of that important day when everyone from the king down participated in joyfully honouring God would remain with even the youngest witnesses.

They'd sought God's direction and followed it. The second time they did things his way and realised his blessing – a timely reminder for us.

In Total Praise

'It was before the LORD, who . . . appointed me ruler over the LORD's people Israel – I will celebrate before the LORD' (2 Samuel 6:21).

Not only is the procession memorable, the installation of the ark in Jerusalem is as well. It is commemorated by public worship and feasting in wholehearted devotion to God and pleasing fellowship among his people. Full of joy, David offers sacrifices to God and then blesses the people in the name of the Lord. God has been gracious to him and he in turn is generous to his people as he gives every man and woman bread, dates and raisins.

The king recites a psalm for the occasion. Through it David reminds the people of God's works, his name, his judgements, covenant and anointing. He urges the people to grasp what God means to do and be to them. David recalls God's acts on their behalf against all odds. He stirs them to testify to God's unique worthiness as creator, Saviour, Lord of history and their source of strength and joy. God alone deserves to be revered and worshipped in holiness and will come again to put things right on Earth.

The song closes with a doxology to which all the people say 'amen' and 'praise the Lord'. The words of the king's song are also found in Psalms 105:1–15, 96:1–13 and 106:1, 47, 48. If David wrote those psalms prior to this occasion, he likely wove portions of them together for the special event.

He entrusts the song to Asaph for the singers of hymns and prayers who give daily service. David appoints Asaph, also a psalmist, as the chief of the musicians. He becomes the father of the clan of musicians who serve throughout the temple's history. After the exile, one of Asaph's descendants was among the first to return to Jerusalem (1 Chronicles 9:15).

Following such an exhilarating day, how unfortunate that when David returns home to bless his family, his wife Michal complains that his dancing in the streets was unsuitable for a king (15:29 and 2 Samuel 6:20)! As daughter of Saul, perhaps she caught the family attitude toward the ark which her father neglected.

David reminds her that he'd rejoiced before the Lord in holy zeal and would continue to celebrate before the Lord. Is God's glory the aim of our expressions of single-minded love for God?

Progeny

'Unless the Eternal builds the house, workmen build in vain' (v. 1, JMT).

When Psalm 128:5 said that the godly would see the good of Jerusalem all their lives, some interpreted that to mean they would make many pilgrimages to Jerusalem.

In Luke 2:41–52 we read of twelve-year-old Jesus visiting Jerusalem with his family for Passover. We imagine that, along with others, he recited some of these pilgrim psalms. In whatever way they sorted themselves – by age, interest or origin – for amiable travel to religious festivals, families regrouped once in Jerusalem. It isn't surprising that some of the pilgrim psalms such as 127 and 128 emphasise God's blessing in domestic life.

Someone has said that most of the world's problems would be solved if everyone had a place to call home. The root word for house, household and house of God is the same. Whether referring to building the temple, a home or a family, the psalmist makes the point that transient human enterprises succeed most lastingly when under divine auspices. 'Eternal' in the key verse accentuates that.

God is the ultimate source of all worthwhile achievement. In the end, human labour without God's blessing is useless. But those who work in co-operation with God can trust that, even in sleep, God works to prosper them.

Some view children as a burden or an inconvenience. Scripture says sons are an inheritance from God and children are to be viewed as a reward, a blessing. Those in family farm or cattle occupations count on family labour. In Old Testament times, progeny meant even more than that. The metaphor of sons as arrows could signify a family's literal defence or its legal one in disputes at the gate where civil cases were decided (v. 5).

As believers, we are God's children, his heritage. 'The Spirit himself testifies with our spirit that we are God's children. Now if we are children, then we are heirs – heirs of God and co-heirs with Christ, if indeed we share in his sufferings in order that we may also share in his glory' (Romans 8:16, 17). We are marked in Christ with the promised Holy Spirit, the guarantee of our inheritance and his (Ephesians 1:13–19). What a hope! All glory to God!

Au Contraire

'You, my God, have revealed to your servant that you will build a house for him. So your servant has found courage to pray to you' (v. 25).

David is settled in his cedar palace and intends to replace the simple tent housing the ark of God with a fitting building. It's an apparently noble goal from sincere motives. The king shares his idea with the prophet Nathan, who concurs and encourages him. Can we blame David that since the scheme is so obviously right to him he doesn't stop to ask the Lord's direction or timing for his undertaking? Haven't we been in similar circumstances?

Fortunately, God speaks to Nathan that night with a reminder and a message for the king. God has been a vital presence with his people wherever they've moved from the days they left Egypt. He initiated the tent of meeting in the wilderness, but never asked any of Israel's leaders to build him a dwelling. God does not want David to build a house for him, rather God promises to build a house for David (vv. 4, 10).

What David plans is a temple. What God confers on David and his offspring is a dynasty with a destiny. It would begin with David, but never end. One day the Son of David would reign over God's kingdom for ever.

God promised Abraham that he and Sarah would be father and mother of nations and kings. Abraham's grandson, Jacob, blessed his son, Judah, with the pledge that kings who would come from his line would anticipate the culminating king, the Messiah. Now David is Judah's descendant and part of the Messianic line.

David's response to God's refusal of his gift shows his godly attitude. As David sits composed before the Lord in prayer, he accepts God's revealed will, thanks him for his promises which have encouraged his prayer, declares God's uniqueness and goodness, asks for God's continued blessing and prays that through God's faithfulness to his word to David and his descendants, people would see how great the Lord Almighty is (vv. 16–24).

To pray:

Lord, teach us to welcome your way and want it more than our own.

A Winning Team

'The LORD *gave David victory everywhere he went' (18:6).*

Immediately after Nathan's restraining prophecy about building the temple, chapters 18–20 summarise the military campaigns that David leads against the enemies of God's people. Perhaps the chronicler puts them here for emphasis since one reason David was not the one to build the temple was that he was a man of war (22:8).

The victories cement David's reputation at home and abroad. The chronicler doesn't give 2 Samuel's graphic detail about David's conquest of Moab, but only says it becomes a vassal state. This may be in deference to David's great-grandmother, Ruth of Moab. The spoils of war from victory over Edom, Moab, the Arameans, Ammonites, Philistines and Amalek increase the royal treasury. David dedicates their gold, silver and bronze to the Lord (18:11), probably anticipating the future temple.

In chapter 18 the Philistines head the list of those David subdues – possibly because they were such a formidable foe. As a young man, not long after God directed Samuel to secretly anoint David as the next king, the first enemy of Israel whom David fought was the Philistine, Goliath. At the end of chapter 20 the chronicler returns to three further conflicts with the Philistines – all centring on giants.

David's reign is noted for justice and judgement (18:14). The growth of his kingdom necessitates administrative organisation. He selects trusted officials. Joab commands the military. Jehoshaphat is spokesman and oversees protocol, Zadok and Ahimelech are priests, Shavsha is a royal correspondent, Benanaiah heads the professional military corps and David's sons are chief officials or advisers (18:15–17).

In the defeat of those who refuse David's overtures for peace, Joab's strategy against the Arameans and Ammonites reveals that David's confidence in him is well placed. He prepares well, but also trusts the Lord for the outcome. He tells his co-commander, 'Be strong and let us fight bravely for our people and the cities of our God. The LORD will do what is good in his sight' (19:13).

More than Numbers

'David replied, "No. I'm buying it from you, and at the full market price. I'm not going to offer GOD sacrifices that are no sacrifice"' (v. 24, MSG).

What could be sinful about statistics? David becomes prey to a ploy of Satan. David's immediate use for fixing a number on the kingdom's population seems to be to calculate the strength of his military machine for further conquests. Perhaps it is to bolster his pride. He may also want to figure out what a taxation could net the monarchy.

God promised that Abraham's descendants would be innumerable. In the many victories the army experienced, David also recognised God's presence and power as more critical than Israel's superior knowledge or might. Whatever David's motives for counting his people, he should have consulted God first.

David's trusted military chief, Joab, objects, not because it's a formidable task but on the grounds that what the king requests will bring guilt on the kingdom. He is overruled. He begins the distasteful task and reports that there are more than a million men eligible for military service.

As happens regularly with David, when he realises he's gone against God's plan he's sorry and asks for mercy. God gives David three punishment options of three durations (vv. 10–12). He chooses the one most dependent on God's mercy, a three-day widespread plague.

Although David's sin results in dire consequences, when he repents and obeys God, God spares the people of Jerusalem and furthers his plan and covenant. A Jebusite gladly offers the king whatever he needs, even though it affects his livelihood. But David understands the value of personal sacrifice when it comes to worship and buys the Jebusite's threshing floor, ox, wheat and even his wooden threshing equipment, then builds the altar there as God directs. God accepts the offering. The plague is stayed (v. 27).

The good that God brings from the king's grave blunder and repentance is that the spot where the future temple would stand is fixed. 'So David declared, "The house of the LORD God is to be here, and also the altar of burnt offering for Israel"' (22:1). What has God fashioned out of our contrition?

Building

'Now devote your heart and soul to seeking the LORD your God. Begin to build the sanctuary of the LORD God' (v. 19).

Television shows devoted to buying, selling, improving or decorating our houses and gardens are popular even with those who aren't planning on any form of upgrade, much less building a home from the ground up. Even building a playhouse or garden shed can be a daunting task for the DIY amateur. How the plans of a key construction project can move from concept to architect's sketch and on through the stages of building to completion amazes us, even when it takes longer than anticipated.

David's cherished dream is to establish the temple at Jerusalem. Since he is not allowed to actually construct the temple, he gathers its considerable building supplies and even the workforce for Solomon to oversee. David's thorough preparation would prevent any shortages or delays in construction.

David charges his son: build the temple as God has directed, rely on God's wisdom in ruling, be faithful to the law of Moses, be strong and courageous and build. 'You're all set – get to work! And GOD-speed!' (v. 16, *MSG*). David reminds the officials of Israel that now the kingdom is at peace, they should stand by and assist Solomon as they had David. He means for the king, officials and people to co-operate and realise his heart's desire – a temple to honour God's name.

God's house is central to Chronicles. In one sense that house can be seen as the whole nation of Israel. In a centralised sense it is the family of David; in the most central sense, it's the temple and the vital faith it symbolises.

Today, The Salvation Army's World Youth Convention begins in Stockholm University's Aula Magna facility. Pray that the delegates will be aware that that building will be to them the temple of God and that the commitments they make there will be considerable and crucial.

To ponder:

'Don't you realise that all of you together are the temple of God and that the Spirit of God lives in you?'

(1 Corinthians 3:16, NLT)

Dedicated Personnel Change Appointments

'And so the Levites carried out their responsibilities for the Tent of Meeting, for the Holy Place and, under their brothers the descendants of Aaron, for the service of the temple of the LORD' (v. 32).

The workers David selects surely chat to each other as they notice the growing heaps of materials he amasses in preparation for the temple. That constant visual reminder must appear considerable and the task formidable. But preparations for the project are not complete until the king arranges for the thousands of people which temple service will require. Chapters 23–26 detail that.

Near the end of David's life, he begins to turn the kingdom over to Solomon. But first, perhaps because of Solomon's relative youth (1 Chronicles 22:5), David organises and plans for the continuation of religion and government for the nation's ongoing good.

We read in 2 Chronicles 3:2 that Solomon began building operations in the fourth year of his reign. We know from 1 Kings 1:32–37 that Solomon became king before David died. Some commentators say that David and Solomon may have been co-regents for as many as four years – allowing for a smooth transition of power.

David counts the Levites aged thirty years and up. Eventually the age of eligibility is lowered to twenty (v. 24). Of the initial 38,000, some would supervise the temple, some would be officials, some gatekeepers and some musicians.

Although all are of Levitical heritage, perhaps many are apprentices, since the ark wouldn't have required such a large dedicated retinue. Even many of those who served with the ark may now have a change in job description in keeping with the needs of the temple (v. 26). They may move from being musicians to assisting the priests by preparing the physical equipment and facility for worship.

David states that the Lord has given the people rest and has come to dwell permanently among them in Jerusalem (v. 25). Although the chronicler is a student of God's acts throughout Israel's history, he is more interested in showing the continuity of Israel's religious faith and God's abiding presence in their midst.

Stewards of Divine Service

'Their fellow Levites were in charge of the treasuries of the house of God and the treasuries for the dedicated things' (26:20).

In three chapters we see a huge organisation of dedicated workers receiving varied assignments and schedules for a smoothly functioning religious core. First David uses two chief priests, Zadok and Ahimelech, descendants of Aaron, to sort the priestly families into divisions. They divide the sanctuary officials impartially, by lot. Due to size, one line carries proportionally more representation. The twenty-four divisions rotate throughout the year.

A scribe registers them in the presence of the king, priest and heads of priestly and Levitical families. The names listed are the founders of divisions which will last for hundreds of years. One of them, Abijah (v. 10), starts the line that Zachariah, John the Baptist's father, comes from (Luke 1:5). Chapter 24 also tells of Levites who are not priests being organised into ministry groups.

In chapter 25 David organises another equally important group – 288 of the 4,000 musicians. They are responsible for 'ministry of prophesying', which probably means they worship God and declare his words and truth through song. These musicians are also sorted into twenty-four divisions. Responsibilities are appointed by lot, which guarantees that there will be no favouritism between young and old, trained and untrained musicians in assigned duties. This could prove an excellent mentoring experience.

Gatekeepers or guards are also on sacred service. According to the list in chapter 26, at any one time twenty-four gatekeepers are on duty. Their placement for duty is also by lot, since certain gates are more prestigious and some more trafficked than others.

Some Levites are managers of the treasury. The temple reserves include offerings from the people and valuable booty and royal gifts designated for temple service or repair.

Magistrates and clerks, perhaps 6,000 strong, are given responsibility 'for administration of matters related to the worship of GOD and the king's work' (26:30, *MSG*) in geographic areas throughout the kingdom. They probably function in rotation as do the other stewards of divine service.

Joy Praises God

'The LORD has done great things for us, and we are filled with joy' (v. 3).

Today's six-verse psalm reflects the joy of returned captives. Their exile was humiliating and devastating. Nebuchadnezzar's invasion and deportation meant loss of their homeland, identity and temple (central symbol of their faith). After Persia took over Babylon, Cyrus's decree of amnesty allowed their return to Judea to begin.

Yet Scripture does not fix blame or credit on either ruler. The names of the kings don't appear. The psalmist knows that the story of God's people is under God's direction as he uses people and situations to accomplish his purposes.

The decree to return seemed too good to be true. No doubt some who longed for release had given up hope, while others who secretly wished for it hadn't expected it in their lifetime. No wonder they thought they were dreaming. Sudden good news can be very disorientating. Did it free emotions and behaviour they'd suppressed? They couldn't bring themselves to sing while their homeland was in ruins and they were in exile (Psalm 137:4). Now they couldn't contain their joy, and sang with full hearts. Others noticed their joy and credited God.

Long before the captivity and God's restoration of the people, Isaiah prophesied just such a day. He wrote to encourage those from Judah to live righteously and hopefully: 'The ransomed of the LORD will return. They will enter Zion with singing; everlasting joy will crown their heads. Gladness and joy will overtake them, and sorrow and sighing will flee away' (Isaiah 51:11).

The grateful exiles had a taste of fresh blessing and asked for more. They weren't satisfied with a trickle, but wanted a stream or the flash flood of a rainy season in the desert. They were eager for all their displaced people to return home. Have we enjoyed spiritual blessings and asked for more? It's not greedy to want what God offers – the fullness of his Spirit for us and others.

The psalm ends with a reminder and a promise. Obedient Christians encounter times of pain and weeping – ours and others'. If even in those times we faithfully carry the word (the seed) and are ready to sow it, ultimately the harvest will come and we will praise God with joy.

Ready

'Be strong in the Lord and in his mighty power' (Ephesians 6:10).

In King David's time, throughout Israel we repeatedly hear some variation of 'Goodbye, take care of each other, I'll be back in a month.' The king organises his military ranks with the same careful attention he gives to his religious forces. For the ongoing needs of state, the militia serves by divisions of 24,000. One division is always on duty, but all can be mustered if needed. Since all twelve tribes supply a division, each is on duty one month a year.

In some reserve forces today, individuals find that such an arrangement means opportunity to serve their country honourably while hardly interrupting their livelihoods. Additionally, in David's time the reserve soldiers probably serve at their own expense or their tribe's, so it doesn't impact the state budget. It is possible that if enough people in a tribe take turns for duty from year to year, service can be shared. In that way more people receive training too.

Most of the names of divisional commanders in chapter 27 are in David's hall of fame heroes list in chapter 11, where several are listed according to their prowess. For example, Benaiah (27:5, 6) was known for overcoming two mighty Moabites, a lion in a pit on a snowy day and an exceptionally tall Egyptian. Under Solomon, Benaiah eventually succeeded Joab as commander-in-chief. Each commander's career sheet would be impressive and revealing.

No doubt all the divisional commanders have assistants – some are named. Serving under these leaders are captains who lead 1,000 men, and under them, leaders of 100. The hereditary rulers over the tribes mentioned in verses 16–22 may hold a quasi-military function, but primarily hold positions of influence as chieftains of clans.

While we are grateful for those who train to serve their country, what of our preparedness as Christian soldiers? In addition to our regular worship, prayer and Bible study, do we intentionally devote concentrated time and resources to honing the weapons of our spiritual armoury so that practising evangelism and holiness becomes our default mode rather than an occasional special emphasis?

The King and Who?

'Your statutes are my delight; they are my counsellors' (Psalm 119:24).

David's organisation of the religious, military and governing bodies for his people is nearly complete. He is careful in all details of preparations before he hands over to Solomon, God's choice as the next king.

Although Saul taxed the people and Solomon would work out a system of support from the whole nation, there is no indication of taxation in David's time. Expenditure is met from the sizeable acquisitions of conquests. As important as the acquisitions are, the effective management and oversight of the royal goods, fields, vineyards, orchards, produce, flocks and cattle is also critical in supplying the considerable ongoing needs of court personnel.

David appoints trusted officers of the court as stewards of his storehouses near and far, his farm labourers, vineyards and orchards and their produce, herds, camels, donkeys and flocks. These care for the state's property.

Before the chronicler ends the list, he includes five other people David relies on and values: Jonathan, Jehiel, Ahithophel, Hushai and Joab. They are, respectively, David's relation who is a man of insight, a counsellor who writes; a tutor for David's sons; a second counsellor; David's friend; and the commander of his royal forces.

We read almost parenthetically that one of these was replaced by others. The back story for this is that he later defected to Absalom, David's rebellious son, and participated in an unsuccessful uprising against David. Ahithophel was succeeded as king's counsellor by Abiathar, the son of the priest who lost his life for helping David when Saul was still king. (See 3 July.) Abiathar proved loyal to David and covertly helped to defeat the defector, Ahithophel.

Most of us reveal something about ourselves by the friends we keep. Those in leadership positions exhibit wisdom by the people they select to assist and advise them. David has good friends and worthy advisers, but learns, as we must, to rely on God above all.

To pray:

We pray that our leaders will seek to discern the truth, choose trustworthy advisers and lead with integrity.

Imperial Organiser

'And you, Solomon my son, get to know well your father's God; serve him with a whole heart and eager mind, for GOD examines every heart and sees through every motive' (v. 9, MSG).

After his extensive preparations for the nation's political, military and religious life, David is ready to see Solomon crowned king. He has already told his leaders of his desire to build a temple and has collected many of the requisite construction materials. Now David's life is near its end and he has a few more things to say.

The fact that we're told he rises to his feet (v. 2) is notable, for at this point David is weak and chiefly bedridden. It adds significance to what he says to his assembled leaders. He tells them that it was his vision to build the temple, but that God had another idea – David's son would build it.

The writer presents the facts of the succession in an unusual way. David reminds everyone that God chose him, but behind that choice, from the twelve tribes, was the choice of Judah and from the families of Judah, the choice of Jesse's family and from Jesse's many sons, David. Now, from David's many sons God's choice is Solomon. Yet the line will not survive unless successors follow God. David's charge in verse 8 is both to the people and his son, then he homes in on his high expectations of Solomon. David gives his successor something in writing, perhaps as his legacy.

We know people who are detail-oriented. They operate best working from lists and think that others do too. Their meticulous plans enable them to accomplish so much and when coupled with the right spirit, bring great blessing to others. If the chronicler is given to detail and functions that way too, it's no wonder that he includes David's comprehensive plans for the temple.

David says that he's written them under the Lord's hand and guidance (v. 19), no doubt based on the earlier tabernacle. David publicly hands Solomon plans for the temple. He includes the priests, the articles to furnish the temple and for use in worship – even down to the amount of gold or silver for each.

Whatever God gives us to do, we can appropriate David's final advice to be strong and courageous because God is with us and know that others around us will help us accomplish God's will (vv. 20, 21).

Exampled

'The people rejoiced at the willing response of their leaders, for they had given freely and wholeheartedly to the LORD. David the king also rejoiced greatly' (v. 9).

David follows up his directive to Solomon about building the temple with a catalogue of the materials he's amassed in preparation. From the resources of his kingdom he provides huge amounts of gold, silver, bronze, iron, wood and precious stones. (In chapter 22 David says he's set aside nearly 4,000 tons of gold and 40,000 of silver.)

Now, in addition, because his heart is in this God-driven project, David discloses he's also dedicating his own personal treasures – more than 100 tons of gold and 200 of silver. Based on his example, he appeals to the whole assembly: 'Now, how about you? Who among you is ready and willing to join in the giving?' (v. 5, *MSG*).

It isn't time for an annual appeal, pledges drive or collection for missions, yet the king's stewards, army officers, heads of tribes and heads of families follow their leader's example and step forward to give willingly to the temple capital campaign nearly 200 tons of gold, 400 of silver, 700 of bronze and 3,800 of iron.

How do the rest respond? 'The people were full of a sense of celebration – all that giving! And all given willingly, freely!' (v. 9, *MSG*). King David is exuberant and breaks into song (today's Scripture reading), then concludes by directing everyone: '"Praise the LORD your God." So they all praised the LORD, the God of their fathers; they bowed low and fell prostrate before the LORD and the king' (v. 20).

David, who probably based his temple plans and calculations on the pattern of the tabernacle, may have recalled that something similar happened when Moses asked the people to bring offerings for the tabernacle. 'Everyone who was willing and whose heart moved him came and brought an offering to the LORD for the work on the Tent of Meeting' (Exodus 35:21). They outdid themselves and had to be restrained from giving more (Exodus 36:6, 7).

Offerings from willing hearts are precious and, when exampled by godly leaders, priceless.

Succeeded

'He died at a good old age, having enjoyed long life, wealth and honour. His son Solomon succeeded him as king' (v. 28).

The day after David's public transmission of the plans to Solomon, the outpouring of giving and David's inspired prayer, a huge animal sacrifice confirms the celebration of the dedication. The people delight in feasting together in the presence of the Lord. In conjunction with the massive celebration and as the last recorded act of David, Solomon is re-anointed king and Zadok as high priest.

Chronicles does not mention the attempted coup by another of David's sons who thought the kingdom should be his. Neither does it mention the former high priest's complicity (1 Kings 1). The original readers would understand that it is at the back of the writer's mind as he emphasises Solomon's legitimate ascension in David's presence.

When the writer states that all Israel obeyed Solomon and that, along with the leaders and chiefs, all David's sons submitted to his authority, he is not glossing over facts but omitting distractions as he chronicles the kingdom from a particular point of view. He wants to leave no doubt about the maintenance of the Davidic line and the construction of the temple. They play a unique role in the divine plan of salvation.

When all is ready, King David dies. David's obituary is brief (as are those of each of the kings the writer details). He states that David was king over all Israel. He doesn't mention that part of the time he ruled only Judah; just that he was king over Israel for forty years – in Jerusalem for thirty-three years and at Hebron for seven.

David attained everything an Israelite king could hope for, definitely a sign that God was with him and blessed him. In spite of his frustration at not building the temple and his disappointment in some of his sons, he knew the blessings of personal forgiveness, of peace in his region, of the respect of world leaders and, most importantly, the presence of God.

David finishes as he began decades before when Samuel described the one God would choose to succeed Saul as 'a man after God's own heart'. May we too be known as such.

Poet Laureate

'You turned my wailing into dancing; you removed my sackcloth and clothed me with joy, that my heart may sing to you and not be silent. O LORD my God, I will give you thanks for ever' (vv. 11, 12).

As we have seen, the political portion of David's line had ended when the chronicler wrote, yet the continuity and legitimacy of David's house was still important to the writer, so he necessarily recounted some of that history. He was given to detail and we learned through him that when it came to administration and planning, David excelled at that as well.

But we might remember David differently from the chronicler, who saw him chiefly as divinely chosen king, although he does attest that David was a singer of songs and the primary organiser of musical guilds for the sanctuary. Jewish tradition, though, remembers David as a writer of sacred poetry and that may be how we think of David.

In 1 Chronicles we notice David's bursts of song at times of jubilation when welcoming the ark to Jerusalem and when publicly turning over the finalised plans for the temple.

In addition, in the book of Psalms, of the ninety psalms with names attached, more than seventy are attributed to David. More than a dozen others contain information about incidents in the life of David, so may be from his heart as well. Today's psalm may have been written in connection with 1 Chronicles 21 after God chastised David and then allowed him to purchase and dedicate the future site of the temple.

In 1 Chronicles we observe David learning lessons of divine guidance that remain instructive for us. Matthew Henry reminds us that David's leadership illustrates that 'those who would draw others to good must lead the way themselves'.

David not only learned valuable spiritual lessons, he shared them. Through songwriting he painted honest word pictures that made the ensuing eternal truths accessible to us. Might we emulate this aspect of David's life by using our varied gifts to confirm God's work in our lives, bless others and bring honour to God?

Above and Around

'As the mountains surround Jerusalem, so the LORD surrounds his people both now and for evermore' (v. 2).

When we think of mountains, depending on our location various images may come to mind. Generally we envision permanent features of a landscape, nearby or distant, which are higher than our everyday surroundings.

Although not the elevation of Blanc, Kilimanjaro, Denali, Fuji, Cristobal Colon or Cook, at about 2,500 feet Mount Zion loomed high in Judah. The psalmist says that trusting in the Lord makes the soul as unshakable as Mount Zion – that lofty Old Testament icon rising as a symbol of all that is stable, solid, perpetual and sought-after. What an image! It is not our trust, but the object of our trust that offers our souls such permanence.

In verse 2 the psalmist keeps the mountain metaphor, but uses it to remind us that not only is God our upward focus, but the One who encompasses us as Jerusalem's other nearby mountains surround the city.

Except to the north, hills or mountains encircled Jerusalem. A city thus surrounded was protected from invasion. The Lord is above, beneath, around his people. While we stay obediently within his circle, we have an impregnable fortress.

The pilgrim psalmist who penned another psalm looked to these hills. When he asked himself where his help came from, the perceptive answer came: 'My help comes from the LORD, the maker of heaven and earth' (Psalm121:2).

In words attributed to Patrick, fifth-century missionary to Ireland, we can affirm:

Christ be with me, Christ within me,
Christ behind me, Christ before me,
Christ beside me, Christ to win me,
Christ to comfort and restore me.
Christ beneath me, Christ above me,
Christ in quiet, Christ in danger,
Christ in hearts of all that love me,
Christ in mouth of friend and stranger.[11]

Amen.

Notable Notes

Philemon and 2 and 3 John

Introduction

They are like choruses rather than songs; succinct postcards rather than lengthy letters; charcoal sketches rather than complex paintings; demo tracks rather than albums. Three of the Bible's shortest books are Philemon, and 2 and 3 John. Although addressed to first-century Christians, they hold truth for us today. This week we'll open them together.

Philemon – Freedom in Christ

Would you find it difficult to write to someone you didn't know well and ask them for a favour? In the briefest of all his letters, Paul seems to write to Philemon with ease. Philemon's reputation for living his faith and demonstrating it in practical ways prepared the way.

Paul writes this letter about the same time as he writes Colossians. The church in Colosse met at Philemon's house. Both letters were sent with the same messengers, Tychius and Onesimus. Paul praises Philemon, pleads for Onesimus and pledges support.

2 and 3 John

Unlike 1 John, which is more of a doctrinal essay full of big themes rather than a letter, 2 and 3 John briefly counsel concerning issues in the early Church's developing organisation. William Barclay says of 2 and 3 John that their very brevity and comparative unimportance indicates their genuineness – no one would have taken the trouble to invent them and attach John's name.

In our Bibles each letter contains scarcely more than a dozen verses. Writing either of them would have required only a single sheet of papyrus – about the size of a piece of today's business stationery. For three days we'll briefly consider them together.

Refreshing Kindness

'Your love has given me much joy and comfort, my brother, for your kindness has often refreshed the hearts of God's people' (v. 7, NLT).

Paul's brief letter to Philemon is unique. He says he writes some of it with his own hand. It's his sole surviving private letter to an individual. The letters he wrote to Timothy and Titus included instruction for the church as well. Here he graciously greets the church, but primarily addresses one person, Philemon.

This is the only letter in which he opens by calling himself a prisoner of Christ rather than an apostle or a servant of Christ. It may indicate that in this case Paul does not appeal to his own authority, but to Philemon's sympathy. In a rare act, Paul plans to ask for a favour, albeit not for himself, but for Onesimus.

Some have criticised him for not addressing the institution of slavery. We imagine that he would like to have done so. Instead he injects a Christian solution into the culture and plants a seed. He advises that despite their station, people should regard each other as equals in Christ and then demonstrates his advice.

As is his custom in letters, Paul tells Philemon that he always thanks God for him when he prays. In Philemon's case it is because of his love for and faith in Jesus and his followers. Paul must have learned of Philemon's attributes through believers who knew him well – such as Epaphras, the Colossian pastor, who was currently in Rome. Even Onesimus may have vouched for Philemon's brilliant life and witness. Paul encourages Philemon to continue to have a generous, Christlike spirit.

Kindness notices my need.
Its gentle voice buoys me up,
stays cheerful through grey days,
doesn't intrude, but draws me out,
encourages me to keep going,
to be grateful, to notice others' needs
and to serve them with kindness.

E. M.

Family Ties

'I appeal to you on the basis of love' (v. 9).

Paul starts in the right place psychologically – with praise for the wronged master. He gives an honest appraisal of the Christian man he hopes to enjoy fellowship with one day.

Paul views a number of those converted through his ministry as family. He says he and his brother Timothy send this letter. At the end of Romans Paul sends greetings to his 'brothers' and other 'relatives' including the mother of Rufus who is like a mother to him. Although rejected by his own family, he entered a wider family of Christ, much as Jesus told his followers would happen (Mark 10:28–31).

Some Salvation Army officers have opened their homes to people as they've ministered to them. Others have borne spiritual children in their own and other cultures. One retired couple hears from people on three continents who consider them their spiritual parents. And from their retirement home they continue to lead neighbours and acquaintances to Christ. Although their physical family is small, their spiritual family is bountiful.

Paul reminds Philemon that he is a senior citizen and imprisoned. On the basis of love, his request is on behalf of his 'son', born in prison. At the end of verse 10 Paul finally names this son, the runaway Onesimus, and then says that he is completely changed – he's beginning to live up to his name ('beneficial') and will prove so for Philemon too.

In Paul's companion letter to God's people at Colosse, he explains why Onesimus will be profitable to his master: 'Slaves, obey your earthly masters in everything . . . with sincerity of heart and reverence for the Lord. Whatever you do, work at it with all your heart, as working for the Lord, not for men' (Colossians 3:22, 23).

As much as Paul would like his 'son' to stay with him, a runaway slave should go home. Keeping him in Rome would be illegal and could be dangerous. Since his Christian ethic teaches oneness in Christ, he asks Philemon to accept the runaway as the brother in the faith that he now is.

How does the family of God keep growing through you?

Expecting the Best of *Koinonia*

'I am confident as I write this letter that you will do what I ask and even more!' (v. 21, NLT).

The way Paul tells Philemon that he's sending Onesimus back implies that he's referring the case to him and the church at his house for a verdict. It's an act of trust. Paul expects that Philemon will freely choose to do the right thing. Considering that the runaway is one of the two messengers carrying Paul's letters, Philemon would have to decide swiftly, without foreknowledge of the situation, when Onesimus appears on his doorstep.

Onesimus must have quickly grown dear to Paul because he says it's heart-wrenching to lose him. He adds that Onesimus could have been Philemon's representative to care for Paul in prison (vv. 12, 13). To reinforce his genuine interest, Paul agrees to pay anything Onesimus owes Philemon. Without dwelling on it, Paul doesn't hesitate to add that Philemon is actually in debt to him (v. 19). Yet he doesn't demand co-operation, but trusts for it.

It is thought that Philemon heard the gospel during Paul's three years in Ephesus (Acts 19:10) – about 100 miles from Colosse. We don't know if that was his first contact with Paul's ministry, but at some point he came to Christ through it.

Besides several others, Epaphras, Philemon's erstwhile pastor, now with Paul in Rome, prays fervently for the Christians at home (Colossians 4:12) and sends his greetings. He must have told Paul about the place where Philemon and Apphia had created an atmosphere of refreshing respite for God's people. Paul says that he hopes one day to visit the oasis at Philemon's house.

Archippus, possibly Philemon and Apphia's son, was probably the pastor in Epaphras's stead. Paul greets him in this letter, and in the companion letter he exhorts him to pay attention to completing the ministry he's been given (Colossians 4:17).

What happened to Onesimus? Did he make a significant local contribution? Did he return to Paul with Philemon's blessing? Is he the Onesimus whom Ignatius later writes about as the great bishop of Ephesus? Whatever developed from his conversion and willingness to go back to make things right, the *koinonia* (fellowship of sharing) would have played a key role.

Balanced Love Knows Limits

'Love means following his commandments, and his unifying commandment is that you conduct your lives in love. This is the first thing you heard, and nothing has changed' (v. 6, MSG).

The letter of 2 John begins as most letters of that day did, stating who the sender is. In this case it's just 'the elder', which could mean either an elderly man or an eye-witness to the life of Christ. No doubt the readers would know who sent it. From style, subject and content, most scholars concur that it is the apostle John.

If the sender's identity seems enigmatic, the recipients' may as well. It's addressed to the chosen lady and her children. Some say this means it's written to a literal woman and her offspring. Other commentators think it is written to a specific church and its members – possibly the church at Jerusalem. In that case, the sister and children who send greetings in verse 13 would correspond with another church and its members – probably the church at Ephesus, where John lives.

John starts with a blessing and an affirmation. They can expect to experience the grace, mercy and peace of God the Father and God the Son. John reminds them how foundational truth and love are to the Christian faith. Since the believers are living out truth, John reminds them that truth's corollary, loving one another, pivots on obeying God's commands and following his will. The test of love is whether it leads us closer to God. Love doesn't acquiesce to sin.

The recipient's charitable spirit is commendable. She welcomes itinerant teachers, common in that day. But she isn't careful about their doctrine. Some teach error and lead believers off course. 'Anyone who gets so progressive in his thinking that he walks out on the teaching of Christ, walks out on God' (v. 9, *MSG*).

John warns that when the Church lacks discernment and opens her fellowship to those who teach false doctrine and exploit her hospitality, it's dangerous. It's true in individual lives too.

What of those who bring veiled counter-biblical messages into our homes through television, radio, movies or print? Do we absorb their principles or check them against the Truth? If we want it and ask him for it, by his Spirit God will give us discernment and wisdom.

On Balance

'They set out under the banner of the Name, and get no help from unbelievers' (v. 7, MSG).

In 3 John, three men are named: Gaius, Diotrephes and Demetrius. John starts by encouraging Gaius, about whom he cares deeply. Gaius may have come to Christ through John. When he hears via others that Gaius puts his belief system into action and continues to walk in the truth, John is justifiably proud and delighted.

Perhaps this friend now struggles with physical challenges. John prays that Gaius's body will prosper as well as his soul does. In a day of Gnosticism, which discounts the body as irrelevant or less important than the soul, John shows his interest in the total person, as Jesus did.

Gaius may have shown hospitality to those who gave John a favourable report about him (v. 3). It is his habit. In 1 Timothy, Paul instructs that hospitality should be a characteristic of Christian leaders. Besides hospitality being an important part of the culture, travelling evangelists depended on the goodwill of those to whom they ministered. Giving to them, some of whom had left homes and jobs to spread the gospel, allowed local believers to contribute to their work in the furtherance of the gospel.

So why does John encourage Gaius to continue to do so? Because there are some disreputable itinerants – charlatans or heretics – John advises discernment (noted in 2 John). But there may also be controversy about the viability of the very concept of itinerant missionaries.

In the first-century Church when this letter is written, the apostles and others have spread the gospel and started churches. At first, roving teachers help to establish and encourage new believers in the faith. In time, in each location, potential local leaders are identified and trained and begin to take responsibility for their churches.

Church organisation is in transition. Some object to the interruption of visiting ministers or even the authority of a mother church – both seen as interferences. Gaius is unsure which approach is correct. Today we, too, need to seek God's guidance and use wisdom in maintaining balanced Christian ministry.

Deflect Diotrephes' Disease

'When pride comes, then comes disgrace, but with humility comes wisdom' (Proverbs 11:2).

Should Gaius prudently offer hospitality to 'fellow workers for the truth' or follow the direction of one of his strong church leaders who insists on exclusivity? Not only does the leader bar travelling speakers from the church and refuse them hospitality, but also insists that others follow his example.

Diotrephes loves and guards his own pre-eminence in the church and openly disdains John's earlier counsel. Such self-centred attitudes can breed stubbornness in others. Strong-minded individuals can easily intimidate. What should Gaius do?

Although Diotrephes may be right in some things, his lack of graciousness and love is unacceptable. Gaius should shun rather than succumb to such spiritual blindness. John advises Gaius not to go along with evil, but imitate what's good.

Straightaway, John provides an example of goodness – Demetrius. He may be a leader of the band of itinerant missionaries, probably John's personal emissary and post-carrier delivering this letter. Typical of a Jewish threefold witness, John says everyone speaks well of Demetrius, his life aligns with truth and John himself vouches for him. Gaius should not hesitate to welcome him.

John hopes to see Gaius soon, probably during a church visit. He'll follow up with Diotrephes then. The prospect of John's visit would encourage Gaius and others. Meanwhile, John prays for his peace and sends the friends in Gaius's church the warm greetings of friends in John's.

Diotrephes' disease continues in fellowships today. His proud resistance, criticism, isolationism and control are still a downward spiral. Are any aspects of such pride evident in our own lives? Do we resist authority, harbour a critical spirit, isolate ourselves from others' instruction or seek to control people?

Jesus teaches about pride's menace in reference to the scribes and Pharisees. His remedy for his followers then and now is: 'The greatest among you will be your servant. For whoever exalts himself will be humbled, and whoever humbles himself will be exalted' (Matthew 23:11, 12).

Delivered

'God's strong name is our help, the same God who made heaven and earth' (v. 8, MSG).

Safe journeys and quiet lives don't make exciting stories. Books, films or television programmes which focus on tragedy or near misses capture our interest. Although we want to know about such dramatic events, we don't want to experience them. What makes us pay attention is not only that they are extreme situations, but that they are so different from what we know in daily life.

What did the psalmist mean by, if it hadn't been for the Lord, the enemy would have eaten Israel alive or swept her away by wild water? Had he known some narrow escapes? Some commentators think the psalm might have been written in thanksgiving for the Jews' last-minute escape from Persian Prime Minister Haman's intended massacre (Esther 9).

Perhaps the writer remembered a time in Israel's history when people were literally swallowed alive, such as when the Earth opened and consumed those who rebelled against God's appointed leaders, Moses and Aaron (Numbers 16). Maybe he recalled when the Red Sea, which had separated into two walls of water flanking the Israelites' path of escape from Egypt, flowed back together and drowned the pursuing army.

Many of us can recall times when we were spared from harm. What witness could we personally add to complete 'if the Lord had not been on our side . . .' (v. 2)? It may be a time years ago when we absolutely knew God literally protected us from harm. Rescue is a miracle. It may be a more current situation when we recognised God's sustaining grace through a stressful time. Take a moment to recollect and thank God again. When we remember God's providential care we can join the psalmist in giving God the credit that we were, literally or figuratively:

> not swallowed alive or washed away,
> not devoured as predators' prey;
> freed from entrapment and harm,
> rescued by God's strong arm (vv. 3–8).

Trees of God's Planting

Introduction

In her 1 June comment, Commissioner M. Christine MacMillan wrote of a young Chinese teen who determined to do his part in counteracting pollution by planting 365 trees in Mongolia – one for every day of the year. The Salvation Army has been involved in tree-planting schemes for decades.

In certain areas of the world, laws are passed to protect trees. Usually this is done in response to a catastrophic loss of trees due to natural disasters, war or unsustainable harvesting or clearing of trees. One company in Asia went beyond using recycled paper when at considerable expense it replaced its cafeteria's disposable wooden chopsticks with a reusable washable type and saved some three tons of wood annually.

We are increasingly aware of the value of trees for our lives and planet and our role in their survival. According to biologists who study satellite pictures of Earth and estimate tree density divided by global population, there are about sixty-one trees per person on the planet.

Scripture frequently refers to trees and sometimes compares believers with them. Whether we're surrounded by trees in full summer leaf or in winter dormancy, in the next days we'll consider trees.

God of the Gallant Trees

God of the gallant trees
Give to us fortitude;
Give as thou givest to them
Valorous hardihood!
We are the trees of thy planting, O God,
We are the trees of thy wood.
Now let the life-sap run
Clean through our every vein,
Perfect what thou hast begun.
God of the sun and rain,
Thou who dost measure the weight of the wind,
Fit us for the stress and strain.

Amy Carmichael[12]

The Plantings of the Lord

'But blessed is the man who trusts me, GOD, the woman who sticks with GOD. They're like trees replanted in Eden, putting down roots near the rivers' (vv. 7, 8, MSG).

Trees are renewable. If you think you're using up more than your allotment, you can always sponsor the planting of a few more. It was ancient Hebrew custom to plant a pine tree at the birth of a girl and a cedar at the birth of a boy.

Several centuries ago in England, aristocrats planted hardwood trees to indicate boundaries of property and their permanent claim to it. Besides its social and political aspects, planting trees was also considered patriotic since the Royal Navy depended on them.

In 2007, Wales began a scheme of planting a native tree to mark each child's birth and to show the family's commitment to a sustainable environment. In one section of Indonesia the government requires a couple seeking approval for marriage to first provide a tree seedling to help reduce deforestation.

Tree-planting schemes are part of Salvation Army programmes in various parts of the world. In Africa, young farmers wanting a loan for a beehive or a goat plant several dozen trees before receiving the loan. Salvationists in India have planted coconut palms around their meeting halls and used income from the nuts to replace benches or roofing.

In a similar way to the familiar Psalm 1, our Scripture passage likens us to a well-planted, watered tree. It's a considerable compliment to be referred to as a tree of God's planting. That's the renown that Isaiah says the Messiah brings those who are his own. When we think of ourselves as God's planting it gives us new perspective on our station and significance in the kingdom.

Where does the Lord plant us? Practically speaking, he plants us in the daily common place where he needs us, and figuratively it's in the house of the Lord for the purpose of proclaiming his righteousness (Psalm 92:13, 15) and the 'display of his splendour' (Isaiah 61:3). Our planet needs more trees and the world needs more plantings of the Lord who reveal the nature of God.

Like a Cedar

'The righteous . . . will grow like a cedar of Lebanon' (Psalm 92:12).

My fascination with plants and trees began as a child when the nature director at summer camp taught me to identify some of them. One of these was the red cedar, commonly called blueberry cedar because of its small bluish cones which look like dusty blue berries. That's the image of a cedar tree in my mind, but there are numerous varieties.

When the Bible speaks of cedar, it's usually the tall cedar of Lebanon. Sometimes enormous in girth and height, they have been used in literature as symbols of strength. When David established Jerusalem and built a palace, King Hiram of Tyre supplied the cedar logs and carpenters. Lebanon cedar was again used in building the temple. It was used for noble purposes. There was no substitute for cedar.

Most cedars are rich grained, fragrant, durable and resistant to insects. Some hold that the cedar's evergreen, beautiful, aromatic, wide-spreading, slow-growing, long-lived and useful characteristics symbolise the Christian.

Believers are called to live for noble, holy service. How can we, who by God's Spirit know new life in Christ, spiritually grow like cedars of Lebanon? We, like the storied cedar, need to respond to stimuli necessary for growth. Additionally, unlike the tree which has no choice about its environment, we can seek aids – means of grace – to keep us maturing in our faith. God will help us.

Ezekiel 17 uses images of eagles and trees in a parable about God's judgement on Jerusalem through the nations which invaded, conquered and carried her into exile. But the chapter's final verses offer hope. There will be a day of restoration and God's glory will be revealed.

The 'shoot' taken from the cedar's crown and replanted is a king from the Davidic line who prospers as a splendid cedar. As a grand tree provides ample nesting places for birds, this king offers safety to those who rest in him. Ezekiel points toward the Messiah in whom alone all who trust for salvation may know safety. Amen.

Tamar

'The righteous will flourish like a palm tree' (Psalm 92:12).

For those who live in a temperate climate, palm trees raise thoughts of the year-round sunshine of a tropical one. The land in which the Bible was written includes temperate, desert and Mediterranean regions which support an abundant variety of plant life. The palm, *tamar* in Hebrew, includes many species. In Palestine the date palm was best known and perhaps most abundant. Its leaves were used in the annual Israelite festival of booths. The familiar scene of Palm Sunday involved leaves from the palm used in a typical way as tokens of victory and peace.

The date palm can grow to heights of 50 feet or more. Although it doesn't bear fruit until it's been planted for six or more years, it can be productive for a century and give some of its best fruit in old age. Its trunk is straight and unbroken. The emerald-green fronds comprising its crown can be as long as 20 feet. The tree has hundreds of uses and the date palm fruit, fibre, leaves and sap are valued.

Many places in the Bible have connection with palms. Soon after the Israelites, recently escaped from Egypt, had gone three days in the wilderness without water and stopped at the bitter waters of Marah, they came to an oasis at Elim where there were twelve springs and seventy palm trees (Exodus 15:27). No wonder they camped where water and shade were abundant.

Jericho was known as the city of palms. During the time of the judges, Deborah, the prophetess and judge, held court under a specific palm tree about ten miles north of Jerusalem (Judges 4:5). Scripture tells us that palms were prevalent in the first temple's decoration (1 Kings 6:29) and in Ezekiel's vision of the future temple (Ezekiel 40, 41).

The palm is upright, verdant, beautiful, elastic and increasingly fruitful and beneficent. It grows steadily upwards and thrives independent of extremes in circumstances – neither teeming rains nor fierce heat cause it distress. These characteristics offer apt comparison with our life in Christ and give pause for thought.

Verdant Praise

'So the people went out and brought back branches and built themselves booths on their own roofs, in their courtyards, in the courts of the house of God and in the square' (Nehemiah 8:16).

As much as palm trees evoke victory, peace and fruitfulness, willow trees may connote lament. We recall that while in exile the Israelites gave up joyful singing and in their sorrow hung their harps on the willow trees by the rivers of Babylon (Psalm 137).

Since willows are fertile and there are many hybrids of the deciduous trees, they are a familiar site near fresh water, especially in temperate regions. Almost all willows take root very readily from cuttings or where broken branches lie on the ground. Strangely, the tree which suggests sadness is the one with bark that provides salicin, precursor to aspirin.

Leviticus records the instruction the Lord gave Moses to pass on to the Israelites regarding annual Jewish feasts he meant them to observe. One of them involved tree branches. 'On the first day gather branches from magnificent trees – palm fronds, boughs from leafy trees, and willows that grow by the streams. Then celebrate with joy before the LORD your God for seven days' (v. 40, *NLT*).

Once established in the Promised Land, they should build temporary booths and live in them for a week as an interactive multi-sensory way of reminding successive generations of their ancestors' transient life in the wilderness and God's grace to them. We note from our key verse from Nehemiah that after the exiles returned from Babylon and rebuilt the walls of Jerusalem they took renewed interest in the word of the Lord and re-instituted their observance of this festival.

We, too, need to remember what the Lord has done in our lives. It may be significant that both palms and willows were used for the booths. We all know times of gladness and sadness. Every life holds such contrasts and not necessarily in equal measure. But we can use them to remind us of God's care through it all and rejoice before him with both our palms and our willows in our worship and our walk before our holy God.

A Tree Fable

'A man's pride brings him low, but a man of lowly spirit gains honour' (Proverbs 29:23).

Tucked away in the book of Judges we find a passage based on one of the Bible's few fables. It uses talking trees as its main characters. Jotham uses his fable to call people to account before God.

The Israelites had offered to make Gideon their king. He refused: 'I will not rule over you, nor will my son rule over you. The LORD will rule over you' (Judges 8:23). But after Gideon's death, one of his sons, Abimelech, thought he should take advantage of the offer. He appealed to his mother's relatives in Shechem to put forward the idea. The Shechemites backed him and gave him money for mercenaries. Then Abimelech slaughtered seventy of his brothers.

Only the youngest, Jotham, escaped. He heard that the Shechemites had crowned Abimelech as king beside a tree and pillar in a place with historical significance connected with Abraham, Jacob and Joshua. So Jotham boldly climbed to another famous location, Mount Gerizim, the mount of blessings (Deuteronomy 11:29), and shouted out his message of prophetic warning in fable form.

The trees decided to set up a king and approached several of their number. They were turned down by the olive based on its rich oil which served God and humankind; by the common fig tree based on its essential fruit; by the vine based on its unique product, wine. Each was fruitful and useful in its appointed place. The cadre of trees literally set their sights continually lower until as final resort they turned to the squat thorn shrub. Useless except for starting fires, it accepted sovereignty and called those who towered over it to take refuge in its non-existent shade or be devoured by its fire.

Jotham prophetically concluded that easily ignited Abimelech would be the cause of civil discord and mutual destruction. By chapter's end, after a brief reign, ironically Abimelech died ignobly while attempting to set a tower on fire. The wickedness of Abimelech and his followers boomeranged.

God's judgements are sure. His mercy extends to those who turn to him in repentance.

Fig Tree

'Yet I will rejoice in the LORD, I will be joyful in God my Saviour' (v. 18).

Today when we say we wouldn't give a fig for something, we're dismissing it as insignificant. But in the Middle East where fig trees thrive in full sun and produce multiple crops of sweet fruit annually, figs have been important. In Bible times, besides being a diet staple, figs had medicinal uses. Canopies of fig trees spread broadly and provided plentiful shade. Jesus used the fig tree in his teaching (*Words of Life*, 6 April 2009) and the tree Zacchaeus climbed for a better view of Jesus was probably a sycamore fig tree.

The fruitful olive and the fig trees are frequently mentioned together in Scripture. They were both in the tree fable in Judges. Moses includes them in his description of the valuable produce the Israelites could expect in the Promised Land. King David appointed an overseer of olive and fig trees. Both were plentiful and vital in the area. When the writer of 1 Kings describes Solomon's wealth, we learn that the king made silver as common in Jerusalem as stones and cedar as plentiful as fig trees in foothills.

Through the prophet Amos, a former shepherd and fig tree tender, the Lord reminded his people that when he allowed the locusts to devour their fig trees, it was to catch their attention, but they hadn't returned to him. Later, through Haggai, God reminded his people that their barren fig trees were meant to bring them back to him and that now they had turned their hearts back to him things would be different. Their continued obedience would enable them to experience God's restoration and blessing.

We may not depend on fig trees, but God still uses loss of what may be regarded as essential to turn hearts to him.

Before either Amos or Haggai's time, when Habakkuk grasped the coming judgement on seemingly unchecked wickedness, he stood in awe of God's power and plans. He was able to declare that even if there were no signs of hope – no fig buds, no olive fruit, no grain, no sheep – he would choose to rejoice in his Saviour.

In seemingly hopeless situations we can be of the same mind as Habakkuk only if we trust our Lord. His Spirit will help us if we ask.

Watching and Waiting

'Like servants, alert to their master's commands, like a maiden attending her lady, We're watching and waiting, holding our breath, awaiting your word of mercy' (v. 2, MSG).

Verses 3 and 4 of this psalm may be a complaint by captives in Babylon when their oppressors treated them with contempt in that foreign land and they had their fill of captivity's hardships. Or the verses may be a cry from returnees to Jerusalem, attempting to restore the walls of their razed city, but mocked by opponents and accused of wrong motives at the outset of their formidable task (Nehemiah 2:19).

But we know that the writer looks hopefully to God. The psalmist says he lifts his eyes to God in heaven (v. 1). Lifting our eyes, looking above and beyond ourselves and our difficulties, demonstrates maturity but lifting our eyes to God in our need shows spiritual discernment. In Proverbs 8:34, 35, Wisdom says: 'Blessed is the man who listens to me, watching daily at my doors, waiting at my doorway. For whoever finds me finds life and receives favour from the LORD.'

The simile in verse 2 of our psalm illustrates how the writer envisioned the stance we take as we wait. I imagine that the best servants are those who make it their business to stay acutely aware of their master's habits, preferences and desires and to be readily available, even at personal inconvenience.

Mary, who became adept at watching and waiting for God, evidences a servant attitude when she graciously accepts Gabriel's startling announcement of God's plan: ' "I am the Lord's servant," Mary answered. "May it be to me as you have said" ' (Luke 1:38).

On the day of Pentecost when Peter powerfully explained God's explosive new enablement, he quoted what years before, through the prophet Joel, God had declared he would do at such a time: 'Even on my servants, both men and women, I will pour out my Spirit in those days' (Acts 2:18).

We are his servants. While we're obeying what we know to do and waiting for God's next instruction we have his inimitable Spirit to keep us alert to evidence of his mercy.

Of the Olive

'To bestow on them . . . the oil of gladness instead of mourning, and a garment of praise instead of a spirit of despair' (v. 3).

Most Holy Land tourists return with a souvenir made from richly grained olive wood. The olive tree was plentiful and indispensable in biblical times. Solomon used its wood for temple doors. Its salt water-cured fruit was eaten, but most olives were collected and pressed or dripped to produce oil for common or sacred use.

A tree could produce half a ton of oil a year. Olive oil was used for cooking then as now, but also for making toiletries, ointments and as lamp fuel. Its most important role may have been connected with worship.

Olive oil was essential in some of the offerings as well as for fuel for the lamps in the tabernacle and then the temple. It was a major ingredient in the fragrant anointing oil used to consecrate Israel's kings and priests for God's service.

In Zechariah two witnesses before the Lord are depicted as olive trees. Their olive oil flows directly into lamps to keep the flame lit. Some conjecture that they might stand for the Old and New Testaments. Most see them representing the dual roles of priest and king which prefigured the Messiah. But the oil is generally considered a symbol of the Holy Spirit, especially since in answer to Zechariah's question about the trees and lampstand the angel gives the word of the Lord about the primacy of his Spirit's empowerment: ' "Not by might nor by power, but by my Spirit," says the LORD Almighty' (Zechariah 4:6).

The Hebrew word meaning 'anointed with olive oil' is from the same root word as 'Messiah'. Yet rather than being publicly anointed as king, Christ went through Gethsemane, literally the olive press, to Calvary to be crushed in our place by the weight of our sin.

In turn, after Christ's resurrection and ascension, God sent his promised Holy Spirit to empower his followers. His oil of gladness comes to those willing to pay the price of following him.

Grafted In

'For there is no difference between Jew and Gentile – the same Lord is Lord of all and richly blesses all who call on him' (Romans 10:12).

A man who loved trees and wanted to foster appreciation for horticulture started a park in California, USA. It includes whimsical arboursculpture. In nature, branches of a tree may graft together in an unusual shape such as a letter of the alphabet. Artist Axel Erlandson let such curiosities guide his experiments in planting trees in patterns that encouraged their grafting to his design.

Unlike topiary, which primarily involves shaping the foliage, arboursculpture entails wounding trees and binding parts together so they grow to a desired shape. Branches may be bent and braced temporarily while new layers of wood grow and become a natural cast.

In Jewish thought the olive tree represented, among other things, renewal – a function of the Messiah. Although olive trees can live to a very old age, older trees are sometimes cut down to make them more fruitful. A new shoot comes from the stump of the old tree and eventually produces healthy branches and fruit. Isaiah used this image when he wrote of the Messiah as the Shoot coming from the stump of Jesse (Davidic line).

Paul reminds us in Romans 11 that Christianity is a branch grafted into the tree of Israel. Judaism is the root that nourished the tree. For a time, God lopped off the unbelieving Jewish branches. And in part because of the Jews' rejection of the gospel, the kingdom came to the Gentiles. Through God's mercy, Christianity, depicted as a wild olive branch, has been grafted into the cultivated tree. This is not a basis of conceit, but of gratitude for grace.

We Christians are indebted to and need our Jewish roots. The Old Testament is groundwork for the New. All true believers are part of the body of Christ. Further, Paul offers hope that Israel will return to righteousness by faith in the manner of their father Abraham and that God will graft his redeemed Israel back in: 'For through him we both have access to the Father by one Spirit' (Ephesians 2:18).

Fruitful Trees

'You didn't choose me, remember; I chose you, and put you in the world to bear fruit, fruit that won't spoil. As fruit bearers, whatever you ask the Father in relation to me, he gives you' (v. 16, MSG).

We have lived in two houses that had mulberry trees in the garden. The first turned the fingers and lips of many neighbourhood children purple while the second, less accessible, attracted only birds. Since the appeal was free fruit, the pickers came in season. Fruit trees are meant to produce fruit.

When the Israelites were about to enter the Promised Land, the Lord instructed them through Moses that when they arrived and planted fruit trees, they should be patient. They shouldn't eat the fruit until the fifth year. Deferred gratification can be difficult, but the Lord promised them a richer crop if they waited (Leviticus 19:23–25).

In Deuteronomy 20, the Israelites were instructed that even during times of war they should not destroy fruit trees in a display of wilful excess but should spare them for their usefulness.

In the Sermon on the Mount, when Jesus reminds his hearers that the fruit people produce in attitude and action demonstrates their true inner qualities, he is warning against false prophets. He says that if a tree doesn't bear good fruit, it will be cut for firewood. But here, and later, he also affirms good trees and good fruit – the transparency of a pure heart.

Bad fruit is as worthless as no fruit. Jesus condemns both. Like a fig tree without figs, a follower of Christ without evidence of his Spirit in his life is judged fruitless. In Jude the writer uses fruitless uprooted trees to describe apostates who ruin the Church's fellowship.

In the Old Testament, due to their false worship, the Lord sent a message of judgement to his people. It included taking away his gifts to them – their harvest and figs and grapes (Jeremiah 8:13). In contrast, when John looks into heaven he sees the tree of life growing with fruit in all seasons (Revelation 22:2). Today the fruit of the Spirit gives us a foretaste of that day (Galatians 5:22–25).

Scent of Water

'Yet at the scent of water it will bud and put forth branches like a young plant' (v. 9, NRSV).

Ten years after an ice storm decimates eastern Canada, a pre-winter storm destroys the north-eastern USA. A tornado, rare to the area, cuts a metres-wide swath through the wooded hills north of New York City. A fire leaves a pine forest a wasteland of charcoal stumps. A shallow-rooted tree blows over in a gust of wind. Whether it took a couple of days or a few minutes, I've seen the ruins freak storms wreak on decades-old trees.

Two of the plagues God brought on Egypt before Pharaoh agreed to the Hebrews' departure involved trees. The hail storm struck everything growing in the fields and stripped the trees. The plague of locusts ate whatever was left, sparing only the area where the Hebrews lived.

Years later Israel's prophets used the destruction of trees as a metaphor in their messages of judgement. Only repentance and return to God could prevent disaster. God said that an Assyrian king's haughty attitude and wilful pride would figuratively kindle a forest fire which would cost him everything. He would have so few trees (soldiers) left that a child could count them (Isaiah 10:19).

God's message through Jeremiah was that judgement on Judah would be like a fierce storm's lightning strike on a choice olive tree, setting it ablaze. He had planted his people, but if necessary would break them down because of their idolatry.

Job contrasts a person's life with a tree's. A felled tree may grow again, but people live only once. It must be said, however, that during our lives the Lord gives us multiple opportunities to turn to him and begin again. Job knew the blessing of a new start.

There is an American elm tree in Oklahoma which speaks of hope. The scarred elm modelled resilience through the fire and debris of the Oklahoma City bombing in 1995 in which hundreds of citizens were wounded and scores killed. The tree's inscription says: 'The spirit of this city and this nation will not be defeated; our deeply rooted faith sustains us.' Could someone say the same of us?

Standing Ovation

'The creation itself will be liberated from its bondage to decay and brought into the glorious freedom of the children of God' (v. 21).

In recent comments we've seen people compared with trees and we recall the blind man Jesus healed near Jericho who at first glance thought he saw people as walking trees.

A sculpture exhibit in an art museum featured trees posed in human-like stances. One bent stump depicted a person crouching, his back covered with butterflies. Sometimes in Scripture, as a literary device, trees are described with human characteristics. We noted that in the fable from Judges.

A woman who had always enjoyed trees found them especially comforting on one particular day. Due to job relocation, the family was moving some distance. Others had gone ahead and she was alone, closing up their home in the northern woods. Pausing for a final look she sadly realised no one was left to say goodbye to her. Movement overhead drew her eyes. The birch trees were swaying in the wind, as if waving a group farewell.

Similarly Isaiah employs metaphors to accentuate times of joy he anticipates when enemies of God's people are defeated. The cedar and pine exult over the demise of the oppressor (Isaiah 14:8).

Isaiah also writes of the marked contrast between Israel and those who worship idols often made of the wood from trees. There's joy in worshipping the living God for who he is and what he's done. He calls all nature, including the trees, to join the praise: 'Burst into song, you mountains, you forests and all your trees, for the LORD has redeemed Jacob, he displays his glory in Israel' (Isaiah 44:23).

Christians know the great joy of sins forgiven through faith in Christ. Isaiah posits the day when the effects of sin are reversed and Messiah finally reigns: 'You will go out in joy and be led forth in peace; the mountains and hills will burst into song before you, and all the trees of the field will clap their hands' (Isaiah 55:12). As Paul tells us in Romans, even creation will rejoice when the Lord our Maker reigns. We pray, work and look for that day when we join the ovation for the King of Kings.

The Tree

'He himself bore our sins in his body on the tree, so that we might die to sins and live for righteousness; by his wounds you have been healed' (1 Peter 2:24).

The New Testament writers often refer to trees. Some references are illustrative, some symbolic and some as background. Through his illustration of the mustard seed, Jesus pointed out how the kingdom of God grows. Something seemingly insignificant can produce exponential growth. The tree, big enough for birds to roost in, comes from a tiny seed. This would encourage the disciples who had only an inkling of what following Jesus would mean.

Since Jesus worked as a carpenter, he would value wood from healthy trees. He used the illustration of the fruitful and unfruitful trees to advise that what we are at the core reveals itself in our lives through character, words and deeds (Matthew 12:33).

On the way to Calvary, when Jesus speaks truth to the women who follow him, he uses a proverb about trees: 'For if men do these things when the tree is green, what will happen when it is dry?' (Luke 23:31). If a vibrant, fruitful tree is felled, what hope is there for the dead tree?

Jesus implies that if he and his message are rejected when he is present, how much more so when he is no longer with them. If an innocent man is condemned by people who claim to revere God, what can we expect when justice and fair judgement are no longer based on divine absolutes?

For our sakes Christ allowed himself to be hung on a tree. Paul refers to the curse associated with hanging on a tree (see Deuteronomy 21:22–23) when he states: 'Christ redeemed us from the curse of the law by becoming a curse for us, for it is written: "Cursed is everyone who is hung on a tree"' (Galatians 3:13). Peter refers to Christ's death on a tree in our key verse as well as in his message to the Sanhedrin in our Scripture reading.

Salvation Army officer Lieutenant-Colonel David Armistead writes: 'In Paradise God planted a tree, whose fruit was picked and halved; in consequence God planted a tree, from which a cross was carved.' Thanks be to God.

Willing Worship, World Peace

'It made me glad to hear them say, "Let's go to the house of the LORD!"' (v. 1, CEV).

Why is Christian worship, the common background to Christian existence, so faithfully and willingly practised? Eugene Peterson says this psalm gives us three reasons: 'Worship gives us a workable structure for life; worship nurtures our needs to be in relationship with God; worship centres our attention on the decisions of God.'[13]

For the psalmist, there was no place like Jerusalem. It was the place of the nation's authority, but more importantly it was the centre of worship. What God had communicated with his people was celebrated there in worship. It helped to make sense of otherwise fragmented lives. Worship still does.

Worship gives us opportunity to obey God by thanking and praising him. It helps us to hear a clear word from the Lord in a context greater than our own circumstances or conditioned viewpoint. Through each thoughtfully chosen aspect of worship we are invited to realign ourselves with God's will for our lives.

Verse 6 in Hebrew contains the pleasing sound of the poet's alliteration of the letter pronounced as 'sh': '*Shaalu shalom yerushalam yishlayu ohabeycha*'. The need for peace in the Middle East is frequently in the news. We may have no other way to help, but we can pray for the peace of Jerusalem.

One commentary says that verses 6 and 7 mean: 'Let peace-including prosperity, everywhere prevail'.[14] We say 'Amen!' When the psalmist tells us to ask God for Jerusalem's peace, he implies that worship should spill out into daily life. Although focal, the sanctuary is not all there is to Jerusalem any more than our places of worship, however humble or grand, are all there is to our towns, cities or nations.

The 'shalom' or heart-peace and well-being mentioned in verse 6 is primarily God's work in lives of individuals. It's what Jesus gave when he healed, forgave or invited a person to follow him. There will be peace in society when there is first peace in our hearts, so let's pray for peace in our hearts, our homes and our world.

Love Elevates

1 Corinthians 8–13

Introduction

We reach for the letter we laid aside several months ago. Paul writes from Ephesus (in today's Turkey), near the south-eastern coast of the island-dotted Aegean Sea. He continues his instruction to the believers a few hundred miles across the sea to the west on the Greek isthmus between two gulfs. Although miles apart geographically and culturally, Ephesus and Corinth shared approximately the same latitude and climate, and today are in the same time zone. Additionally, Paul had spent considerable time in Corinth so could easily visualise the believers' circumstances.

Although the thrust of the letter deals with particular issues that arose in a particular place during the early days of the Church, Paul's inspired epistle reveals many timeless principles and raises questions we do well to consider personally.

For a time in the modern Church, discovering individual spiritual gifts was a popular exercise. Perhaps you have taken a spiritual gifts inventory too. It can be interesting and affirming. But Paul encourages us to remember that the important thing is not which gifts we have, but that we are actively obeying and serving the Lord in building up his Church.

Paul starts 1 Corinthians 8 by recognising that we all have knowledge, but that knowledge inflates whereas love elevates. The final chapter we consider amplifies that point. We will spend several days with the well-known Love Chapter, so reading 1 Corinthians 13 in several versions could be a helpful complement to the daily comments. Let's pray that the Lord will show us something fresh even from this well-known chapter.

Free to Eat

'But food does not bring us near to God; we are no worse if we do not eat, and no better if we do' (v. 8).

When we laid aside this letter a few months ago, we finished with comments on chapters 6 and 7 in which Paul gave instructions about Christian liberty and advice in response to the Corinthians' questions about marriage. He now turns to another specific issue Corinthians faced – eating meat.

Today's discussions on whether to eat all, some or no meat often revolve around health or social conscience concerns. What does it do to my body or how does the way it's raised and killed impact the animals and the employees who handle the meat?

The first-century issue Paul addressed was different. The Corinthian Christians were split over the acceptability of eating meat which had come from a pagan temple. There were many gods and temples in Greece. Animal sacrifices abounded. No doubt the air in Corinth was full of odours of roasting meat.

What wasn't used in the burnt sacrifice was cooked for special holiday meals at the temple. When there was more than needed for rituals, sometimes leftover meat went to the marketplace. Anyone could buy it, perhaps at bargain prices. Should a Christian overlook its source and eat it?

Paul starts by recognising that we all have knowledge. Corinthians would agree with that. But he continues by saying that knowledge inflates whereas love elevates. Then he hurries to his point. We who know the one true God know that idols are nothing, since the gods they represent are nothing. So eating food related to them is harmless and not immoral.

But since some believers were so used to thinking of anything related to an idol as evil, they couldn't bring themselves to eat the meat. Paul does not, of course, advise knowledgeable Christians to abandon freedom in favour of prejudice or injustice. Hoping that weaker individuals will mature into Christian liberty, showing love for others should always take priority over insisting on our rights in any arena.

Free to Refuse

'Our decision all along has been to put up with anything rather than to get in the way or detract from the Message of Christ' (v. 12, MSG).

At the close of chapter 8, writing about employing or curtailing freedom, Paul says he'd be willing to be a vegetarian for the sake of keeping another believer from faltering. Now in chapter 9 he shows how he personally applies the principle.

He refuses to be supported by those to whom he ministers so that he can't be blamed for wrong motives. He says that as an apostle he has 'rights' (same word as 'freedom' in 8:9). His rhetorical questions in verse 1 about his ministry set the stage for asking if the church should not then support him.

He gives illustrations from various walks of life where those providing service are customarily supported. A soldier doesn't have to provide his own food. Those who raise crops or tend flocks benefit from the results of their labour. Christian soldiers, church planters, shepherds, too, should be able to expect support from those who benefit from their efforts.

But Paul and Barnabas purposely don't cash in on this. Paul says he prefers to sacrifice such rights so that he doesn't cut into (literal translation for the word 'hinder') the work of the gospel. He's seen what happens when those in religious service use position or privilege for personal gain.

To avoid being a stumbling-block by appearing that he's in ministry for the benefits and thus discrediting his message, he prefers not to take even what is due to him. Was he stubbornly principled?

A local council was given the authority to release funds that would potentially increase benefits to thousands. No one could dispute such a magnanimous deed. Everyone supported it. But two Christian members thought the effective date should be delayed. Immediate implementation would make them beneficiaries and it could appear that their judgement had been motivated by personal gain. They preferred that the policy only commence after they would no longer qualify. They followed Jesus' example of sacrificial servant leadership. Paul would have cheered.

Free to Adapt

'I've become just about every sort of servant there is in my attempts to lead those I meet into a God-saved life' (v. 22, MSG).

Besides avoiding any hint of mercenary interest, Paul says he restricts his rights so that he can minister freely and from his heart. His enthusiasm to preach the gospel comes from his dramatic conversion. His ministry is his stewardship of Christ's saving grace.

A Salvation Army officer takes his guitar to the street when he collects funds. He plays songs about the Lord. One dismissive young man taunts in passing, 'I'll give you twenty dollars if you play Led Zeppelin.' The captain breaks into a tune from the rock band and wins the donation. More important than credibility from anyone listening, he gains a hearing for the gospel.

Paul was willing to twist himself into almost any shape to be enough like his hearers to gain a hearing. Yet, as Wesley Harris writes in one of his imaginary letters to the apostle Paul: 'Identification without Christian identity would have been fruitless, but you managed to maintain the critical balance.'[15]

Or as *The Message* paraphrases what Paul says in the first part of our key verse: 'I didn't take on their way of life. I kept my bearings in Christ – but I entered their world and tried to experience things from their point of view.'

That type of evangelism takes bold creativity. Such a daring, seemingly spontaneous manner can be daunting, especially to more reserved personalities. But God knows us intimately and asks us only to be willing to do what his Spirit prompts us to do. His guidance is well suited.

We begin in the right place if we pray with early-day Salvationist Frederick Booth-Tucker:

O give me a heart that is true,
Unspotted and pure in thy sight,
A love that would anything do,
A life given up to the fight!

(*SASB* 422)

Free to Trust

'Don't be so naive and self-confident. You're not exempt. You could fall flat on your face as easily as anyone else. Forget about self-confidence; it's useless. Cultivate God-confidence' (v. 12, MSG).

In chapter 8 Paul shows that if we excessively emphasise freedom, we can place a stumbling-block in a new believer's path. In chapter 9 he explains that putting our 'rights' above everything else, even if we think our efforts or stations merit them, can hinder the effective spread of the gospel. In chapter 10 he warns that promoting personal liberty can have negative effects even to our own Christian walk.

His warning in the first ten verses comes through illustrations, instances from Israel's history. God delivered his people from Egypt and blessed them with spiritual and physical guidance, food and drink, but many turned from him and fell into sin. Whether through indifference or over-confidence, they displeased God in numerous ways and he had to punish them. Paul says the principle of the Old Testament example continues to apply to the Corinthians and it does to us as well.

Privilege does not guarantee victory. It can lead to the opposite – a callous attitude toward spiritual things. Perhaps the Hebrews took God's blessings and presence for granted and the wonder wore off.

Besides over-confidence, some of the Corinthians were tending toward relapsing into idolatry. In the first century that was related to festivals that honoured idols. For us that can mean anything that displaces devotion to God in our hearts.

Satan delights in any enticement he can use to drive a wedge between us and God. Sin allows Satan a foothold, and then he accentuates it. Those who claim that liberty allows an occasional foray into morally questionable areas are especially vulnerable.

We pause to ask the Lord to show us if there are areas we need to address personally, sins we need to confess and forsake. We know that he is willing and able to forgive us, cleanse us, restore us and keep us. He's waiting for us to ask him.

Free to Follow Christ

'So whether you eat or drink or whatever you do, do it all for the glory of God' (v. 31).

Paul gives further attention to the pressing issue for the Corinthians – when to eat what with whom. He says everything is permissible, but hurries to add that not everything permissible is beneficial or constructive. He isn't talking about cross-contamination in food preparation. We need to think about what benefits our spiritual health and what builds up the health of others.

He's already said believers could follow their Spirit-sensitised conscience and eat whatever was sold in the market, even if that was temple leftovers. He hasn't changed his mind, but adds that if for some reason a fellow diner points out that since the meat came from temple remainders, in good conscience he can't eat it, it would be best for the stronger Christian to skip the meat this time too.

Libertarians might find such behaviour restricting. 'For why should my freedom be limited by what someone else thinks? If I can thank God for the food and enjoy it, why should I be condemned for eating it?' (vv. 29–30, *NLT*).

Paul advises, in activities which are neutral – not moral or immoral – and left to individual Christian conscience, the underlying guiding principle should not be 'What do I want?', but 'What will benefit others?'; not 'What will others think?', but 'What will most honour God?'

Paul led the way in freedom. Before his conversion, as a Pharisee, a zealous, law-loving, formalist Jew, he had tried to stamp out Christianity. Faith in Christ brought him freedom from external trappings of human rules and religious practices. Yet he was willing to restrict his personal freedoms for the sake of the gospel.

He urges Corinthian Christians to follow his example and be considerate of Jews, Gentiles and fellow believers so that their behaviour doesn't hinder ministry to the unsaved or the saved. In the first verse of chapter 11 Paul points to his ultimate example and ours, Christ.

Free, Not Independent

'For as woman came from man, so also man is born of woman. But everything comes from God' (v. 12).

Paul expresses appreciation that the Corinthians had heeded his earlier advice, and then he deals with another issue – headgear for public worship. We don't know how it came up. Perhaps it was a consequence of Paul's teaching of all things made new in Christ. A few years earlier he wrote to Christians in Galatia: 'For all of you who were baptised into Christ have clothed yourselves with Christ. There is neither Jew nor Greek, slave nor free, male nor female, for you are all one in Christ Jesus' (Galatians 3:27–28).

Corinthians sometimes took their freedoms to extremes. Perhaps some women assumed that they were free from usual customs of head covering. Or perhaps the underlying issue was wilful pride at the expense of consideration for others or reverence for God. Commentators advise that the Greek grammar in verse 6 indicates a deliberate indifference toward modesty and custom.

Paul advises men to worship with uncovered heads. Jewish men usually covered their heads for prayer, as did Romans. Except for slaves, Greek men did not. It seems that Paul favoured the Greek position on this. He wasn't trying to foist new behaviour on them.

For women he preferred head coverings, in part because of what a bareheaded woman suggested in those days. Paul adds that his direction is common practice. We remember that the people to whom he wrote lived in a licentious city and that believers appearing too modest was preferable to appearing shockingly lax.

It's noteworthy that Paul doesn't dispute whether a woman can speak or pray in public worship, but only whether she should meet with conventions of modesty and respect.

Paul advocates the partnership of deference in the roles of the married man and woman. Further, footnotes in *The Woman's Study Bible*[16] suggest the relationship between redeemed man and woman should reflect the nature of relationships within the Godhead and God's relationship to his Church. Even during Jesus' incarnation and willing subordination, Father and Son were equal while carrying out different roles.

My Soul's Keeper

'My help comes from the LORD, who made heaven and earth!' (v. 2, NLT).

We may see hills or mountains and feel inspired by the scenery. In the days of the psalmist the hills were also full of the oddities of pagan worship – a shrine, a seer, a charm or the favour of one god or another for sale. No wonder when the psalmist looks at those hills he asks where his help comes from. So whether thinking of the majestic view or the shrines of charlatan priests, he concludes that looking to the hills won't bring real help.

Help comes from the Maker of heaven and earth. Wherever we focus our gaze fills our vision. Today's visitors to Jerusalem's Eastern Orthodox churches see numerous icons. The apparent flatness of their images is intentional so that the eye of the viewer is drawn not into the painting, but upward to God.

In *The Great Stone Face*,[17] Nathaniel Hawthorne tells the tale of a boy called Earnest in the White Mountains of New Hampshire, USA. His town was near a lake in the shadow of the Old Man of the Mountain, a 40-foot-high naturally formed stone profile of a man's face jutting out against the sky 1,200 feet above the lake. Ernest regularly looked at the rugged face with the desire to see the fulfilment of a legend – that someone who looked like the stone face would one day come to the town. Meanwhile he lived a simple, hardworking and loving life. Years later it turned out that Ernest himself was that man with chiselled features.

Perhaps not physically, but spiritually we start to resemble what we focus on. I cannot be a living icon deflecting the gaze of others from me to the Lord unless I'm looking to him myself.

The Lord who is never off guard keeps his people, day and night. His interest does not wax and wane. He cares about our daily needs as well as our eternal salvation. We face the same pressures and troubles as non-believers, but we are not left to our own devices or to seek answers for our daily needs from today's gods of the hills, whether media, entertainment or self-indulgence – poor substitutes for God's truth.

With gratitude we say with Salvationist songwriter Eric Ball: 'You are here, Lord Jesus, Christ of my every day.'

Seasoned with Grace

We thank you, Lord, for this our food, much more because of Jesus' blood. Let manna to our souls be given, the Bread of Life sent down from heaven.
(A table grace)

In some churches, all who attend Sunday-morning worship are welcome to stay for a meal. This is especially helpful to the elderly and anyone who travels from a distance. Some pastors are intentional about building the fellowship of believers through arranging times to share food regularly and other experiences together. It's not unusual to see a church-wide family meal on the monthly church schedule.

In Paul's day, before the development of the ritual patterned on the Last Supper, the shared meal was usually pot-luck style. It concluded by focusing on Jesus' sacrifice.

Through practical application of Christ's teachings, the early Church relieved some of the social problems that government couldn't manage. Social differences should have melted away when everyone shared from what they could contribute to a common meal. Within the strict boundary lines of society of that day, it was the one place people could expect to be on equal footing with those of other levels of society.

But Paul criticises the Corinthian Christians for wasting their opportunities at such meals by separating into exclusive factions of similarly opinionated and like-situated people. They abused time meant for a feast of fellowship with other believers and a pledge of fidelity to Christ.

Earlier in the chapter Paul addressed an issue which possibly stemmed from a misunderstanding – female modesty at worship. But perversion of the common meal and remembrance of Christ's sacrifice was a subject of heavy import and revealed unfortunate divisions within the congregation. In this they were doing more harm than good (v. 17).

Do we prepare thoughtfully and gather intentionally for Christian worship and fellowship? Do we season such times with grace?

Out of One, Many

'Like good stewards of the manifold grace of God, serve one another with whatever gift each of you has received . . . so that God may be glorified in all things through Jesus Christ' (1 Peter 4:10, 11, NRSV).

From the way Paul begins chapter 12 with 'now concerning spiritual gifts', we sense that he is addressing another question the Corinthians raised via either letter or messenger. Paul isn't discussing God's gift of his Spirit to believers or the fruit of his Spirit produced in us, but the gifts or instruments of the Spirit which God uses through us to help the Church.

There are different kinds of gifts, ministries and activities. We note that all of them stem from God. In verses 4–6, when Paul mentions all three Persons of the Godhead he accentuates the unity in the Godhead related to the gifts. They are Spirit-given, Christ-honouring and under the Father's auspices.

Just as the gifts all come from one source, they are given to one end – the common good of building up the body of Christ: 'A spiritual gift is given to each of us so we can help each other' (v. 7, *NLT*). The spiritual gifts Paul mentions in his letter to the Corinthians reflect what is happening in the Church. The list is not exclusive. Additional gifts are listed in other epistles. Through the Church God continues to show his many-sided wisdom in its infinite variety (Ephesians 3:10).

Here Paul mentions wisdom, knowledge, faith, healing, miraculous powers, prophecy, ability to discern between spirits, speaking in an unlearned language and interpretation of the same. These seem to have been essential in the establishment of the early Church.

The point of 1 Corinthians 12 is not so much about discovering our gifts as it is about being prepared to serve others and finding that, as we do so, God gives us what we need, often in natural concord with our abilities, interests and tendencies. Using whatever gifts we have for the sake of others often brings us the bonus blessing of fulfilment.

Being satisfied with whatever gifts we have honours the Giver. Using the gifts glorifies God. Amen.

Christ's Body, Vital

'Now you are the body of Christ, and each one of you is a part of it' (v. 27).

We've heard that if, while sitting, you draw clockwise circles in the air with your right hand and then counter-clockwise circles with your right foot, involuntarily your hand will also change direction. Perhaps all our body parts aren't as obviously tied together.

A normal body comprises many parts. In his description of some of those parts Paul does not say they are all the same, but that they are all essential. Their differences underscore their interdependency. God, their Maker, cherishes them all.

The Spirit of Christ gives life to the body of Christ, the Church. A thousand well-organised parts may comprise an effective organisation, but only the Holy Spirit who draws us to Christ and his cross can regenerate us individually and place us in the body where each individual Christian makes an unequivocal difference to the whole.

We are all valued; none is more important than the other in the body because: 'By means of his one Spirit, we all said goodbye to our partial and piecemeal lives. We each used to independently call our own shots, but then we entered into a large and integrated life in which *he* has the final say in everything . . . Each of us is now a part of his resurrection body, refreshed and sustained at one fountain – his Spirit – where we all come to drink' (vv. 8–13, *MSG*).

Who is it shows me what to be
And leads me to that goal?
Who is it claims the heart of me
And wants to take control?
Who is it calls to holiness
Of body, mind and soul?
That's the Spirit! Holy Spirit!
That's the Spirit of the Lord in me!
John Gowans (*SASB* 204)

Christ's Body, Visible

'You are Christ's body – that's who you are! You must never forget this. Only as you accept your part of that body does your "part" mean anything' (v. 27, MSG).

Paul lists some of the gifts believers receive. He may have chosen to intentionally name them in the order he did. He may have been reminding the Corinthians that, contrary to their assessment, those who ministered as apostles, prophets and teachers used gifts that were important to the growth of the whole church.

Corinthians may have preferred the more dramatic gifts which entailed self-expression. But Paul would next pay tribute to what is needed most in any church: love.

Our place in the body of Christ brings both privilege and challenge. In a poem from his unpublished collection of poems, *To His Glory*, Salvation Army officer Commissioner Harry Read reminds us of this:

The Body of Christ

Christ is our risen and ascended Lord
And reigns in glory at the Father's side;
His earthly mission done, his love outpoured,
His place in heaven enhanced, his name adored.
But this our world is not bereft of Christ!
The much-loved ministries he exercised
Will by his followers be realised.

For God in his great wisdom has decreed
That through the Holy Spirit's energies
We who are his will, by our thought and deed,
Express where'er we are Christ's ministries.

We are Christ's body in this world today
And must his mind and heart and deeds display.

Christ's Body, Vibrant

'So you should earnestly desire the most helpful gifts. But now let me show you a way of life that is best of all' (12:31, NLT).

Paul valued the variously distributed spiritual gifts, but knew that no matter which gifts different believers received individually, God wanted to produce his own traits in every Christian. The fruit of the Spirit rectifies squabbles over gifts.

Paul may have deliberately placed chapter 13, the Love Chapter, in the midst of chapters of correction in contrast to the way Christians were treating each other in Corinth. The danger of people with different gifts ranking those gifts or seeking others' gifts interrupts the function of the body. Only one thing can bind all members together in unity and advance the Church – the spirit of love.

There have been many paraphrases of 1 Corinthians 13. For example, from his experience as an international emergency responder, Major Daryl Crowden paraphrases verse 3: 'If I deliver everything promised and in the process completely exhaust myself, but have not love, I gain nothing. I can build the best houses, and dig the deepest wells, but if I have not love, and I do not offer dignity and respect, I am only a service provider.'[18]

Possibly we could spend time writing our own versions by substituting what we esteem in place of the things the Corinthians prized: speaking many languages, understanding spiritual mysteries, exercising miracle-working faith or sacrificial giving.

The bottom line is that without God's love, our very best is not enough. Retired General John Gowans emphasises the best gift:

> Now the fruit of the Spirit is patience,
> And the fruit of the Spirit is peace,
> The fruit of the Spirit is gentleness
> And joy that will never cease.
> The gift of the Spirit is healing,
> And hope for the darkest hour,
> The gift of the Spirit is love, yes, love
> And power, and power.
>
> (*SASB* chorus 46)

A Hymn of Love

'Three things will last forever – faith, hope, and love – and the greatest of these is love' (v. 13, NLT).

Paul shifts from first to third person, from what he would be without love to a personification of love. In verses 4 to 7 of what some call a hymn of love, Paul catalogues sixteen qualities.

Love is patient. We're told that the word Paul uses for patience indicates patience with people, not situations. Christian love expressed as patience with people, especially those who aggravate us, is a powerful testimony and reflects the patience Jesus exhibited with his disciples and demonstrates with us.

As we continue with the characteristics of love, we understand why some have called the chapter a portrait of Christ. Love is kind – consider Jesus' attitude toward the woman taken in adultery. Love is happy for others rather than envious of their blessings. Love neither pushes itself forward before others nor inflates its own ego, even privately.

The Corinthians may have especially needed this particular reminder, since the word translated 'proud' in verse 4 appears six times in this letter. The word's root comes from bellows and means 'to puff or blow up, to inflate'.

Verse 5 continues with four things love is not – rude, self-seeking, easily angered or a score-keeper of others' wrongs. Paul saw some of these negative behaviours in the way the Corinthian believers treated each other. Perhaps we find some of these tendencies in ourselves.

Rather than finding pleasure with unrighteousness and injustice, especially with respect to what others experience, Paul states in verse 6 that love rejoices with truth.

Love bears all with triumphant fortitude and without resentment. Love doesn't spotlight others' imperfections. Love believes the best of others; but when disappointed, hopes for better things; then holds its ground even when it can no longer believe or hope.

Does this sound impossible? Such love can come only from its source: God. When we intend to please him in our living and loving and depend on his enabling Spirit, he will help us to love like Christ.

Where Else but to God?

'I took my troubles to the LORD; I cried out to him, and he answered my prayer' (v. 1, NLT).

This is the last psalm we consider in the set of pilgrim songs or songs of ascent (Psalms 120–134). They were sung by people streaming to Jerusalem for annual feasts and they assist us on our spiritual pilgrimage heavenward as well.

Dissatisfaction with the deceptions of the world around us can help us want something better. The writer of today's psalm is in that state. All is not right with his world and he senses he's been deceived. We all have been.

When the global economy's downward spiral affected millions who lost jobs or possessions, some acknowledged the deception of reliance on the primacy of wealth and what it could buy. It was a wake-up call about values, and for some a turning point.

Repentance is like that too. We come to realise that humanity is not self-sufficient and society's frenzied activity is misguided. We are not our own masters and our harried or dull lives lack direction. Saying no to the world's lies and yes to God's truth about ourselves is the beginning of a pilgrimage. Do you remember when you came to such a turning point, the start of your spiritual journey?

Sadly there are many around the world who live in the midst of war or its consequences. We pray for their deliverance and peace. It is not likely that the psalmist literally lives among barbarous people, but uses Meshech and Kedar symbolically for people in his life who thrive on strife and deceit.

We may not live in the throes of war, but we know how it feels to be misunderstood, lied about or confused by others' thoughtless, selfish or hurtful speech or actions. None understands that better than Christ. He will help us keep a godly spirit if we ask him.

The psalmist's opening declaration demonstrates his testimony as well as his confident continued determination to take his troubles to the Lord. That was a fitting place to begin in the initial psalm of ascent. As our last Sunday psalm in this edition, it is also a suitable place to close.

Christian Identification

'Dear friends, we are already God's children, but he has not yet shown us what we will be like when Christ appears. But we do know that we will be like him, for we will see him as he really is' (1 John 3:2, NLT).

After Paul outlines the importance and excellence of love, he finishes by describing its permanence. Love is eternal. Even wonderful gifts which help bring the Church to maturity are only temporary. When they've accomplished their purposes, they will one day become obsolete.

Paul gives two illustrations about love's fullness or completeness. First he says that, as an adult, he's packed up behaving as a child in speech, thought and reasoning (v. 11). He may have mentioned these three things particularly to parallel the three gifts the Corinthians prized which he'd pointed out earlier – prophecy, tongues and knowledge (v. 8). They were admirable, but not to be seen as ends in themselves or badges of spiritual achievement.

Corinth manufactured metal mirrors which needed to be polished frequently with an abrasive to keep them shiny enough to reflect a discernible image. The Corinthians would have grasped Paul's illustration comparing seeing an unclear image in a cloudy mirror with not seeing a clear spiritual picture. Things that puzzle us won't become clear until the day we see Christ in person.

Paul declares that of the three things that last – faith, hope and love – love is supreme. For now, faith and hope are expressions of love. William Barclay says: 'Love is the fire which kindles faith and it is the light which turns hope into certainty.'[19] When the object of faith in Christ and hope for a future are realised in his presence, faith will be replaced by seeing and hope by knowing. Only love will never end.

Love is the mark Christ gives us to wear. If we exhibit and practise love, especially when we have differences with other believers, it both identifies us as Christians and lets the world know that God sent Jesus (John 13:34; 17:21). What an amazing result! May God help us faithfully to wear his identifying mark.

Love Cannot Fail!

'Love never fails' (v. 8).

If we listen thoughtfully to the poignant words and melody of 'Love Cannot Fail'[20] (a paraphrase of 1 Corinthians 13) we will determine again to know and have and give the love of God freely:

If I could understand the hidden mysteries of life,
If I could know the secrets all men seek,
If I could know the reason why the world is what it is,
Why ev'ry human being is unique . . .
Unless I knew the love of God, the all-embracing love of God,
Unless I knew the love of God, I would know nothing,
I would know nothing!

If I could hold the wealth of all the world within my hands,
Possess the priceless treasures of the earth,
If all the precious things that men have prized belonged to me,
And lovely things of unimagined worth . . .
Unless I had the love of God, the all-embracing love of God
Unless I had the love of God, I would have nothing,
I would have nothing!

If I should spend my strength to build a better world than this,
And spoke of brotherhood with ev'ry breath,
If I should give my goods to feed the children of the poor,
And for my faith would die a martyr's death . . .
Unless I gave the love of God, the all-embracing love of God,
Unless I gave the love of God, I would give nothing,
I would give nothing –

But I will give the love of God,
The all-embracing love of God,
But I will give the love of God.
Love cannot, Love cannot,
Love cannot fail!

John Gowans

Notes

1. *The Complete Collected Poems of Maya Angelou*, © 1994, Random House, Inc., New York.
2. William Barclay, *The Daily Study Bible Series: The Gospel of Mark*. St Andrew Press, Edinburgh, 1954, revised and updated by St Andrew Press, 1975.
3. *Nelson's Bible Commentary*, © 1962, Thomas Nelson & Sons, New York.
4. *New Living Translation*, second edition, © 1996, 2004 by Tyndale Charitable Trust.
5. *Renovation of the Heart in Daily Practice* (6 September 2006), © NavPress, Colorado Springs, CO, USA.
6. *Beacon Bible Commentary, Vol. III*, © 1967 Beacon Hill Press of Kansas City, Kansas City, USA.
7. *The Autobiography of Prayer*, Albert Edward Day, © 1952, Kessinger Publishing, LLC 2007.
8. *Christianity Today*, 6 January1997, 'When Prayer Doesn't Work'.
9. *Called to be God's People* is The Salvation Army's Spiritual Life Commission's report. A revised edition published in 2008 by International Headquarters is available from Amazon.co.uk
10. John Coutts, *Saints Alive – a Brief History of the Christian Church*. Salvation Books, The Salvation Army International Headquarters, London, UK. © 2008 The General of The Salvation Army (available from Amazon.co.uk).
11. Adaptation of a portion of *St Patrick's Breastplate* set in metre in 1889 for *The Irish Church Hymnal* by Cecil Frances Alexander.
12. Amy Carmichael's poem appears in the devotional compilation, *Springs in the Valley*, Mrs Charles E. Cowman, 1997, Zondervan, Grand Rapids, Michigan, USA.
13. Eugene H. Peterson, *A Long Obedience in the Same Direction*, © 1980 InterVarsity Press, Downers Grove, Illinois, USA.
14. Jamieson-Fausset-Brown Bible Commentary.
15. Wesley Harris, *Dear Paul*, Salvation Books, The Salvation Army International Headquarters, London, UK. © 2008 The General of The Salvation Army.
16. *The Woman's Study Bible* (NKJV), © 1995 Thomas Nelson, Inc.
17. *The Great Stone Face*, published in 1852 as part of the final collection of Hawthorne's short stories: *The Snow-Image, and Other Twice-Told Tales*. Copyright 1899 and 1902 by Thomas Y. Crowell & Co.

18. *The Officer*, January–February 2009, The Salvation Army International Headquarters, London, UK. © 2009 The General of The Salvation Army.
19. William Barclay, *The Daily Study Bible Series: The Letters to the Corinthians*. St Andrew Press, Edinburgh, 1954, revised and updated by St Andrew Press, 1975.
20. From the musical, *Spirit*, John Gowans and John Larsson. Copyright © The Salvation Army (1974). http://www.gowans-larsson.com/Spirit/Lovecannotfail.html

Index

May–August 2010

(as from January–April 2005)

Subscribe...

Words of Life is published three times a year: January–April, May–August and September–December

Four easy ways to subscribe

- By post – simply complete and return the subscription form below
- By phone – +44 (0)1933 445 445
- By email – mail_order@sp-s.co.uk
- Or visit your local Christian bookshop

SUBSCRIPTION FORM

Name (Miss, Mrs, Ms, Mr)..
Address ....
....
.... Postcode ....
Tel. No...
Email* ....

Annual Subscription Rates
UK **£10.50** *Non-UK* £10.50 + £3.90 P&P = **£14.40**
Please send me .... copy/copies of the next three issues of *Words of Life* commencing with **September 2010**

Total: £ .... I enclose payment by cheque ☐
Please make cheques payable to *The Salvation Army*

Please debit my Access/Mastercard/Visa/American Express/Switch card

Card No. ☐☐☐☐ ☐☐☐☐ ☐☐☐☐ ☐☐☐☐ **Expiry date:** ___ /___

Security No. ☐☐☐ **Issue number (Switch only)** ______________

Cardholder's signature: .... **Date:** ....

Please send this form and any cheques to: **The Mail Order Department, Salvationist Publishing and Supplies, 66–78 Denington Road, Denington Industrial Estate, Wellingborough, Northamptonshire NN8 2QH, UK**

☐ *We would like to keep in touch with you by placing you on our mailing list. If you would prefer not to receive correspondence from us, please tick this box. The Salvation Army does not sell or lease its mailing lists.